Visual-Spatial Thinking

for **ADVANCED LEARNERS**

Grades 3–5

Visual-Spatial Thinking for Advanced Learners, Grades 3–5 will teach students how to perceive and represent visual information, and to mentally manipulate objects within space.

Visual-spatial thinking is a skill which helps students develop depth, complexity, and abstraction in thinking and inquiry. Working through the lessons and handouts in this book, students will develop spatial language, learn to visualize and mentally manipulate visual information, look at objects from varying perspectives, explore dimension, and seek structure in organizing visual information. This curriculum provides cohesive, focused, scaffolded lessons to teach each targeted area of competency followed by authentic application activities for students to then apply their newly developed skill set.

This book can be used as a stand-alone gifted curriculum or as part of an integrated curriculum. Each lesson ties in both reading and metacognitive skills, making it easy for teachers to incorporate into a variety of contexts.

Emily Hollett and **Anna Cassalia** are award-winning gifted educators and instructional differentiation coaches with Williamson County Schools, Tennessee.

Discover the other books in the Integrated Lessons in Higher Order Thinking Skills series

Available from Routledge
(www.routledge.com)

Analytical Thinking for Advanced Learners, Grades 3–5
Emily Hollett and Anna Cassalia

Convergent Thinking for Advanced Learners, Grades 3–5
Emily Hollett and Anna Cassalia

Divergent Thinking for Advanced Learners, Grades 3–5
Emily Hollett and Anna Cassalia

Evaluative Thinking for Advanced Learners, Grades 3–5
Emily Hollett and Anna Cassalia

Visual-Spatial Thinking

for **ADVANCED LEARNERS**

Grades 3–5

Emily Hollett
and
Anna Cassalia

Routledge
Taylor & Francis Group

NEW YORK AND LONDON

Cover image: © Educlips

First published 2023
by Routledge
605 Third Avenue, New York, NY 10158

and by Routledge
4 Park Square, Milton Park, Abingdon, Oxon, OX14 4RN

Routledge is an imprint of the Taylor & Francis Group, an informa business

© 2023 Emily Hollett and Anna Cassalia

Library of Congress Cataloging-in-Publication Data
A catalog record for this title has been requested

ISBN: 978-1-032-21347-7 (hbk)
ISBN: 978-1-032-19923-8 (pbk)
ISBN: 978-1-003-26794-2 (ebk)

DOI: 10.4324/9781003267942

Typeset in Warnock Pro
by Deanta Global Publishing Services, Chennai, India

Access the Support Material: www.routledge.com/9781032199238

We would like to dedicate this book to all the students we have taught and will teach. You are the reason why we love this profession and wrote this series. We would also like to dedicate this series to our families, who have supported us unconditionally.

Contents

Acknowledgments   ix

Preface   x

	Introduction to Visual-Spatial Thinking	1
	Materials	1
	Introduction: Frame of the Discipline	1
	Primary Source: Artwork Analysis	5
	Thinking Skills Avatar	8
	Bibliography	8
Chapter 1	Sub-Skill 1: Spatial Language	9
	Spatial Language Lesson 1: Language of Position	10
	Spatial Language Lesson 2: Language of Movement	19
	Spatial Language Authentic Application Activity:	
	Reflections and Symmetry	26
	Spatial Language Concluding Activities	37
	Bibliography	38
Chapter 2	Sub-Skill 2: Visualizing	39
	Visualizing Lesson 1: Mental Manipulation: Tangrams	40

Contents

Visualizing Lesson 2: Mental Manipulations:
Pentominoes   54

Visualizing Authentic Application Activity: Visual
Puzzle-Palooza   63

Visualizing Concluding Activities   87

Bibliography   88

Chapter 3   Sub-Skill 3: Visual Perspectives   89

Visual Perspectives Lesson 1: Viewpoints   90

Visual Perspectives Lesson 2: Seen and Unseen   94

Visual Perspectives Authentic Application Activity:
Illusions   103

Visual Perspectives Concluding Activities   113

Bibliography   113

Chapter 4   Sub-Skill 4: Exploring Dimensions   115

Exploring Dimensions Lesson 1: Building 3D Shapes   116

Exploring Dimensions Lesson 2: Comparing
Dimensions   128

Exploring Dimensions Authentic Application Activity:
The Math of Origami   150

Exploring Dimensions Concluding Activities   162

Bibliography   163

Chapter 5   Sub-Skill 5: Seeking Structure   165

Seeking Structure Lesson 1: Coordinate Grids   166

Seeking Structure Lesson 2: The Four-Color Theorem   179

Seeking Structure Authentic Application Activity:
Euler's Circuits   186

Seeking Structure Concluding Activities   194

Bibliography   196

Appendix A: Assessments   197
Appendix B: Extensions   211

Acknowledgments

Special credit and acknowledgment must go to the many individuals whose work has paved the way for current educators like ourselves.

We draw great inspiration from the work of Sandra Kaplan, Alex Osborn, Sydney Parnes, Tamra Stambaugh, and Joyce VanTassel-Baska, whose curricular frameworks and research into best practice for teaching gifted learners are a driving force in shaping our own work.

Our guiding principles are grounded in National Association for Gifted Children (NAGC) programming standards, and we are so thankful for this organization's tireless dedication to gifted students, advocacy, and lifelong learning.

Clipart courtesy of Educlips. Used with permission under an extended license for hard copy books.

Handout font courtesy of Kimberly Geswein. Used with permission under a single font license.

Preface

The *Integrated Lessons in Higher Order Thinking Skills* series provides explicit instruction, targeted problems, and activities to teach gifted and high-ability students how to think using convergent, divergent, analytical, evaluative, and visual-spatial reasoning.

This unit was developed by and for teachers of gifted and advanced learners to provide explicit instruction in higher order thinking skills. In today's ever-changing, fast-paced world, our students require skill sets beyond rote memorization. Vast research supports the development of higher order thinking skills, including both creative and critical thinking skills which go beyond basic observation of facts and memorization. Systematically teaching these processes to students develops their ability to use these skills across the curriculum, building their ability to be "thinkers"—the ultimate goal of education.

The term "21st Century Thinking Skills" is widely used in education today, and while definitions vary, most educators agree: we need to be teaching our students not just *what* to think, but *how* to think. Learners in the 21st century must possess an array of thinking skills. They must be inquisitive about the world around them, and willing to ask questions and make mistakes. They must be logical and strategic thinkers. Logical thinking requires students to clarify problems while analyzing and making inferences based on the given information. Strategic, or deliberate, thinking requires students to think about where they are now in the learning process versus where they want to be in the future, and then determine action steps to achieve their goals.

Gifted and high-ability students require specialized instruction which is organized by key concepts and overarching themes. They need content which requires abstract thinking on a higher level than what is typically required by the general education curriculum. Beyond this, they require time to grapple with meaningful problems and derive defensible solutions. The *Integrated Lessons in Higher Order Thinking Skills* series provides scaffolded, focused lessons to teach these skills and give students authentic opportunities to develop these vital thinking processes.

Rationale

As Tony Wagner (Wagner and Compton, 2012) noted, our current educational system is obsolete and failing to educate our youth for the world of tomorrow. Wagner (Wagner and Compton, 2012) stated, "Students who only know how to perform well in today's educational system—get good grades and test scores and earn degrees—will no longer be those who are most likely to succeed. Thriving in the twenty-first century will require real competencies far more than academic credentials" (p. 20). Our educational system must help our youth discover their passions and purpose in life, and then develop the crucial skills necessary to think critically and creatively, communicate effectively, and problem-solve (Wagner and Compton, 2012).

Developing 21st-century thinkers requires a classroom environment that welcomes cognitive discourse and embraces the growth mindset approach. We must also teach our students that it is acceptable not to have an immediate answer; that some questions have many possible solutions, and indeed, some may never be answered; that persevering and being able to admit what you don't know is an important piece of learning.

Today's students must use metacognition, or awareness of and reflection on thinking processes. Metacognitive thinking is abstract in that one must analyze their thinking processes. Examples of this type of thinking might be asking oneself: "How did I get to that answer?" or "Where did my thinking go off track?" Learning to analyze the process of thinking is vital to problem-solving and learning. Teaching metacognitive strategies is a powerful way to improve students' self-efficacy, depth of thinking, and inquiry skills.

Students of the 21st century must develop problem-solving skills which require both creative and critical thinking. Creativity is a divergent thought process which involves generating new and unique possibilities. Critical thinking is a thought process which involves examining possibilities using a systematic, constructive method. Our students will be faced with unforeseen challenges that they must be able to think about creatively, critically, and strategically to solve. We, as educators, cannot possibly teach students everything there is to know, as the amount of new information available in the world is multiplying rapidly. Therefore, we must teach students to be inquisitive, analytical, innovative, evaluative, and curious. Learning and applying these thinking skills will prepare our students to solve the problems of tomorrow.

While we know the importance of higher order thinking, it is often left behind the "testable subjects" such as reading, writing, and arithmetic. This series was created to merge higher order thinking skills and the academic content students must grapple with in school. Systematic instruction in higher order thinking skills coupled with rigorous academic content is a relevant and engaging method to teach the students of the 21st century.

Higher order thinking consists of several distinctive and sophisticated thought processes. Central to these processes are the areas of systematic decision making (deductive reasoning), evaluative thinking, divergent (creative) thinking, concept attainment and rule usage (analytical). In addition, visual-spatial reasoning has emerged as one of the most important skills for developing overall academic expertise, especially in technical fields. Each of these central processes is addressed in its own book within the *Integrated Lessons in Higher Order Thinking Skills* series.

Focus Strand: Visual-Spatial Reasoning

Visual-spatial reasoning is a crucial 21st-century thinking skill involving perceiving, explaining, and representing visual information. Although spatial reasoning skills and competencies are identified critical components of the National Council for Teachers of Mathematics *Principles and Standards for School Mathematics* (NCTM, 2000), the National Research Council points out that it is often "presumed throughout the K-12 curriculum but is formally and systemically taught nowhere" (National Research Council, 2006). This unit seeks to explicitly teach these essential skills, making them accessible to students while providing a level of challenge appropriate for gifted learners.

Spatial thinkers are able mentally manipulate objects within space, thinking critically about how objects relate to one another and taking on a variety of unique perspectives. This unit is unique in that it allows students to engage in productive struggle while learning to reason visually and spatially. Working through the lessons in this book, students will learn strategies and specific academic vocabulary in five distinctive visual-spatial sub-skills, applying each of these skills to new and complex challenges. The goal of this unit is to help students learn to mentally manipulate visual information while thinking critically and flexibly.

Students will learn visual-spatial reasoning strategies in the sub-skills of developing spatial language, visualizing, manipulating visual perspectives, exploring dimension, and seeking structure. Each of these skills is taught explicitly through three lessons, increasing in complexity and abstraction, and culminating in an application lesson and activity. This approach allows students to build their visual-spatial thinking skills incrementally and apply each skill as it develops. By completing all lessons in this book, students will be able to apply visual-spatial reasoning skills and strategies to a variety of problems, situations, and contexts.

Conceptual Framework

This curriculum is targeted for third through fifth grade gifted and high-ability students. Each of the five Thinking Skills units will provide students ways to develop problem-solving skills which require both creative and critical thinking. Frameworks for questioning and methodology were drawn from several research-based sources, including the Depth and Complexity Framework (Kaplan and Gould), Visual Thinking Curriculum (Tishman, MacGillivray, and Palmer), and the National Council for Teachers of Mathematics Principles and Standards.

Working through the lessons in this book, students will make connections by thinking in ways that incorporate elements of the Depth and Complexity Framework, such as thinking like a disciplinarian, connecting to universal themes, reasoning using question stems derived from the icons/elements, and examining problems through the lens of the content imperatives. Students will learn the visual-spatial specific academic vocabulary. Students will learn to visualize and mentally manipulate visual information. Students will also look at objects from varying viewpoints learning about perspective and illusions. Students will explore dimensions through visualizing and constructing objects from multiple perspectives. Finally, students will learn to order and organize visual information based on patterns and rules. Visual thinking routines are also incorporated to help scaffold students' metacognitive processes. Each of these research-based frameworks is embedded within the lessons in the form of question stems, instructional processes, graphic organizers, and methodology.

Each unit in the series uses explicit instruction to directly and systematically teach students how to think. Research shows that the most empirically supported method for teaching critical thinking is explicit instruction (Abrami, Bernard, Borokhovski, Wade, Surkes, Tamim, and Zhang, 2008). Using explicit instruction makes the learning outcomes clear.

Students are provided with clear, specific objectives. The unit lessons are broken down into manageable chunks of information. The teacher models the thinking skill with clear explanations and verbalizes their thinking process. Students are taught specific ways to reason and problem-solve. Students then practice the skills while the teacher provides feedback. At the conclusion of each lesson, students are asked to think metacognitively about their own learning.

Lesson Format and Guidelines

Each *Integrated Lessons in Higher Order Thinking Skills* unit follows the same format. Students are introduced to the higher order thinking skill through introductory lessons and materials to build schema in the targeted thinking area addressed in the unit. The introductory lesson in each unit provides a real-world connection. The overarching thinking skill is then broken down into five sub-skills. Each sub-skill is explicitly taught in three lessons. First, the students will be introduced to the sub-skill using an anchor chart. Then, students will participate in a warm-up activity teaching the sub-skill. Next, students will read and analyze trade books which highlight the sub-skill. Finally, students will participate in an activity learning to use the sub-skill. The third lesson in each sub-skill provides an opportunity for the students to apply the sub-skill in an authentic application activity. Key features of this unit as well as lesson summaries are outlined in Table P.1.

Unit Features

Materials

Included in this book are blackline masters of consumable materials to be used with students. Student handouts are provided with each lesson, and they include reading reflections, graphic organizers, full text stories for collaborative learning activities, formative "exit tickets," and others. Teacher materials, including anchor chart posters to provide visual cues for sub-skills, detailed lesson plans, and assessment rubrics, are also included. Other needed and optional materials are listed in lesson outlines. Links are provided for online resources, such as short video clips, and are accurate at the time of this book's printing.

Throughout the unit, trade books are used to teach and explore sub-skills in familiar contexts. These carefully selected trade books provide an exemplar for the lesson's focus. The recommended books are common and easily accessible; however, alternate texts are recommended to target each sub-skill (see Appendix B). Many of the texts may also have a digital version readily available as an online read aloud, accessible through a quick internet search.

TABLE P.1

Unit Overview

Introduction and Rationale Teacher introduction providing rationale for the unit.	❑ Outline of Thinking Skills: Teacher reference explaining an overview of each thinking skill and outcome. ❑ Standards Alignment: Unit alignment to both CCSS and NAGC standards are outlined.
Thinking Skill Overview This section provides introductory lessons and materials to build schema for students in the specific targeted thinking skill addressed in the unit.	❑ Frame of the Discipline: Think Like an Architect ■ Students gain understanding of authentic uses for visual-spatial skills within a career context. ❑ Artwork Analysis: Students analyze a piece of classic visual art through the lens of visual-spatial thinking to build thinking skill schema. ❑ Thinking Skills Avatar: Provides an ongoing touchstone for students to record key details and synthesize learning throughout the unit

Sub-Skill 1: Spatial Language
In this section, students will develop the skill of using precise academic vocabulary to describe spatial relationships, positions, and movements.
	❑ Lesson 1: Language of Position
	  ■ Students work with scenes and objects to accurately describe positions of objects in space.
	❑ Lesson 2: Language of Movement
	  ■ Students practice transformational geometry.
	❑ Authentic Application Activity: Reflections and Symmetry
	  ■ Students create quilt squares with rotational and reflectional symmetry.

Sub-Skill 2: Visualizing
In this section, students will learn to create pictures in their minds and mentally manipulate visual information.
	❑ Lesson 1: Mental Manipulation: Tangrams
	  ■ Students apply problem-solving strategies and spatial reasoning through manipulating tangrams to solve interesting puzzles.
	❑ Lesson 2: Mental Manipulation: Pentominoes
	  ■ Students apply transformational geometry to develop spatial reasoning using pentominoes.
	❑ Authentic Application Activity: Visual Puzzle-Palooza
	  ■ Students apply their understanding to a variety of novel visual puzzles.

Sub-Skill 3: Visual Perspectives
In this section students analyze various visual points of view and visual illusions.
	❑ Lesson 1: Viewpoints
	  ■ Students learn how the angle of viewing affects one's observations.
	❑ Lesson 2: Seen and Unseen
	  ■ Students work collaboratively to gain understanding of how many viewpoints create a complete image.
	❑ Authentic Application Activity: Illusions
	  ■ Students will learn how the eyes work with the brain to take in visual information.

(Continued)

TABLE P.1
(Continued)

Sub-Skill 4: Exploring Dimensions
Students will develop an understanding of the different dimensions through constructing and deconstructing 2D shapes and 3D solids.
	❏ Lesson 1: Building 3D Shapes
	  ■ Students construct three-dimensional structures using two-dimensional plans, exploring the connections between dimensions.
	❏ Lesson 2: Comparing Dimensions
	  ■ Students deconstruct three-dimensional shapes into two-dimensional nets using their knowledge of geometric concepts and visualization skills.
	❏ Authentic Application Activity: The Math of Origami
	  ■ Students apply their knowledge of dimensions to make connections between math and paper folding.

Sub-Skill 5: Seeking Structure
Students learn how to order and organize visual information using patterns, repetitions, and rules.
	❏ Lesson 1: Coordinate Grids
	  ■ Students use the structure of the coordinate grids to uncover mystery pictures.
	❏ Lesson 2: The Four-Color Theorem
	  ■ Students learn how cartographers use order to organize visual information.
	❏ Authentic Application Activity: Euler's Circuits
	  ■ Students will investigate connections and pathways using the structure of Euler's Theorem.

Appendix A	❏ Assessment Options
Appendix B	❏ Extension Options

In addition, some lessons utilize common classroom manipulatives such as attribute blocks, pattern blocks, or Tangrams. Printable versions of these manipulatives are also provided as handouts where they are used.

Teacher's note: It is always recommended that teachers preview any content (books, videos, images, etc.) before implementing it with students. Be sure to consider the context of the classroom and/or school in which the materials are to be used, being sensitive to the needs, experiences, and diversity of the students. Where possible, alternate trade books are suggested. Links provided are known to be accurate at the time of this book's publication.

Assessments

Possible *answer keys* and suggested *key understandings* are provided throughout the unit. These sample answers were created to help the teacher see the intended purpose for each lesson and illustrate the thinking skills students should be mastering. However, due to the open-ended nature of many of the lessons and activities, these answers should only be used as a guide and variations should be encouraged.

Blackline masters of assessment options are provided in Appendix A. Formative assessments are provided throughout the unit in the form of an exit ticket to conclude each sub-skill section. An overall unit rubric is provided along with diagnostic guidelines for observation. A whole-group checklist is provided for each sub-skill with diagnostic guidelines included. Teachers should review and select assessment options that best meet their goals for their students. It is recommended that students be formatively assessed on the thinking skills as this an ongoing process and all progress should be celebrated and acknowledged.

Time Allotment

Each lesson in this unit is intended to be taught in 60–90 minutes, but some lessons may take less or more time. In general, this unit can be taught in 15–20 hours of instructional time.

Unit Goals and Objectives

Concept

To develop conceptual awareness of visual-spatial thinking skills using cross-curricular lessons, the students will:

- ❏ Apply visual-spatial academic vocabulary
- ❏ Visualize and examine structures using various perspectives
- ❏ Understand the different dimensions
- ❏ Understand how to organize visual information

Process

To develop visual-spatial reasoning, students will learn to:

- ❏ Perceive and represent visual information
- ❏ Mentally manipulate objects within space
- ❏ Visualize and examine structures through various perspectives

❏ Explore dimension
❏ Look for repetitions and patterns to organize visual information

Standards Alignment

Common Core State Standards (CCSS)

Standards are aligned with each of the five thinking skills targeted in the series *Integrated Lessons in Higher Order Thinking Skills*. Specific thinking skills are noted using the following key (see also Table P.2):

❏ A: Analytical Thinking
❏ C: Convergent Thinking
❏ D: Divergent Thinking
❏ E: Evaluative Thinking
❏ V: Visual-Spatial Thinking

NAGC Programming Standards Alignment

Teaching thinking skills aligns with NAGC Gifted programming standards as best practice for gifted students:

❏ **Standard 1**: Students create awareness of and interest in their learning and cognitive growth
❏ **Standard 2**: Thinking skill aligned assessments provide evidence of learning progress
❏ **Standard 3**: Explicit instruction in thinking skills and metacognitive strategies is research-based best practice and meets the needs of gifted students for opportunities to develop depth, complexity, and abstraction in thinking and inquiry
❏ **Standard 5**: Competence in thinking skills promotes cognitive, social-emotional, and psychosocial development of students

TABLE P.2

CCSS Alignment

Language Standards	CCR Anchor Standards for Reading *1, 6, 7, 8*	❏ Draw logical inferences from text (C/E) ❏ Cite text evidence to support claims (C/E) ❏ Assess perspectives (A/C/D/E/V) ❏ Evaluate various content formats (A/C/D/E/V) ❏ Evaluate arguments based on evidence (E)
	CCR Anchor Standards for Writing *1, 3, 4, 8, 9, 10*	❏ Write arguments, citing text evidence and using valid reasoning (C/E) ❏ Write narratives (D) ❏ Develop written work appropriate to a variety of tasks (A/C/D/E/V) ❏ Evaluate and synthesize information from a variety of sources (E) ❏ Draw evidence to support analysis (A) ❏ Write routinely and for many purposes (A/C/D/E/V)
	CCR Anchor Standards for Speaking and Listening *1, 2, 3, 4*	❏ Collaborate for a variety of purposes with a variety of partners (A/C/D/E/V) ❏ Integrate information from a variety of sources (A/C/D/E/V) ❏ Critically evaluate speakers' perspectives (E) ❏ Present information, including evidence, in ways that allow others to follow lines of reasoning (A/C/E)
	CCR Anchor Standards for Language *3, 5, 6*	❏ Make effective use of appropriate language in a variety of contexts (A/C/D/E/V) ❏ Understand and make use of figurative language (A/D/E) ❏ Develop and apply academic vocabulary (A/C/D/E/V)
Mathematics Standards	CCSS for Mathematics: Practice Standards	❏ Make sense of problems and persevere in solving them ❏ Reason abstractly and quantitatively ❏ Construct viable arguments and critique the reasoning of others ❏ Model with mathematics ❏ Use appropriate tools strategically ❏ Attend to precision ❏ Look for and make use of structure ❏ Look for and express regularity in repeated reasoning *Applicable to problems presented in all Thinking Skills units.*

(Continued)

TABLE P.2
(Continued)

	CCSS for Mathematics: Operations and Algebraic Thinking *2.OA, 3.OA, 4.OA, 5.OA*	❏ Generate and analyze patterns and relationships (A/C/V) ❏ Represent problems both concretely and abstractly (A/C/V)
	CCSS for Mathematics: Measurement and Data *2.MD, 3.MD, 4.MD, 5.MD*	❏ Represent and interpret data (A/C/V)
	CCSS for Mathematics: Geometry *2.G, 3.G, 4.G, 5.G*	❏ Solve problems involving the coordinate plane (V) ❏ Solve problems involving lines, angles, and dimensions (V) ❏ Reason with shapes and their attributes (V)

Bibliography

Abrami, P. C., Bernard, R. M., Borokhovski, E., Wade, A., Surkes, M. A., Tamim, R., and Zhang, D. (2008). Instructional interventions affecting critical thinking skills and dispositions: A stage 1 meta-analysis. *Review of Educational Research*, 78(4), 1102–1134.

Common Core State Standards Initiative. (2022a) Common core state standards for English language arts & literacy in history/social studies, science, and technical subjects. http://www.corestandards.org/wp-content/uploads/ELA_Standards1.pdf.

Common Core State Standards Initiative. (2022b) Common core state standards for mathematics. http://www.corestandards.org/wp-content/uploads/Math_Standards1.pdf.

Dweck, C.S. (2006). *Mindset: The new psychology of success*. New York: Random House.

Golomb, S.W. (1994). *Pentominoes*. Princeton, NJ: Princeton University Press.

Kaplan, S. and Gould, B. (1995, 2003). *Depth & complexity icons, OERI, Javits project T.W.O. 2. Educator to educator. LVI*. J. Taylor Education, 2016.

Levine, M.D. (2009). Differences in learning and neurodevelopmental function in school-age children. In W.B. Carey, A. C. Crocker, W.L. Coleman, E.R. Elias, H.M. Feldman (eds), *Developmental-Behavior Pediatrics*, Fourth Edition. (pp. 535–546). W.B. Saunders,.

NAGC Professional Standards Committee (2018–2019). 2019 Pre-K-grade 12 gifted programming standards. https://www.nagc.org/sites/default/files/standards/Intro%202019%20Programming%20Standards.pdf.

National Research Council. (2006). *Learning to think spatially: GIS as a support system in the K-12 curriculum.* Washington, DC: National Academies Press.

National Council of Teachers of Mathematics. (2000). *Principles and standards for school mathematics.* Reston, VA: National Council of Teachers of Mathematics.

Park, G., Lubinski, D., and Benbow, C. (2010). Recognizing spatial intelligence. *Scientific American.* https://www.scientificamerican.com/article/recognizing-spatial-intel/.

The birth of graph theory: Leonhard Euler and the Konigsberg bridge problem. *Science and Its Times: Understanding the Social Significance of Scientific Discovery.* Enclycolopedia.com: https://www.encyclopedia.com/science/encyclopedias-almanacs-transcripts-and-maps/birth-graph-theory-leonhard-euler-and-konigsberg-bridge-problem.

The Mathematics and Laws Behind Crease Patterns. https://origami.me/crease-pattern-theory/

Tishman, S., MacGillivray, D., and Palmer, P. (1999) Investigating the educational impact & potential of the MoMA'a visual thinking curriculum. http://www.pz.harvard.edu/projects/momas-visual-thinking-curriculum-project.

Wagner, T., and Compton, R. A. (2012). *Creating innovators: The making of young people who will change the world.* New York: Scribner.

Introduction to Visual-Spatial Thinking

Key Question: What is visual-spatial reasoning?

Materials

- ❏ Handout I.1: Visual-Spatial Thinking: Do It Like an Architect! (one per student)
- ❏ Handout I.2: Framing the Thinking of an Architect (one per student)
- ❏ Primary Source Artwork: *A Sunday Afternoon on the Island of La Grande Jatte* by Georges Seurat (display digitally using the link provided)
  - ■ https://www.artic.edu/artworks/27992/a-sunday-on-la-grande-jatte-1884
- ❏ Handout I.3: Primary Source: Art Analysis (one per small group of students)
- ❏ Handout I.4: Visual-Spatial Thinking Avatar (one per student)

Introduction: Frame of the Discipline

- ❏ Tell students they will be learning how to think using visual-spatial reasoning. Visual-spatial reasoning involves perceiving and representing visual information. It also includes mentally manipulating objects within space.
- ❏ Read together the article "Visual-Spatial Thinking: Do It Like an Architect! (Handout I.1).

DOI: 10.4324/9781003267942-1

Handout I.1: Think Like a Disciplinarian

Visual Spatial Thinking: Do it Like an Architect!

Name: _____

Architects are people who design all kinds of structures. They design houses, skyscrapers, bridges, and hospitals. Architects are responsible for developing creative designs that are aesthetically pleasing to the eye, functional, and safe. They need to make the building structurally sound which means it is strong and stable. The structure must be designed to be functional for the people using it. Architects use their **visual/spatial** skills along with math, art, science, technology, and engineering to build structures and buildings. **Visual/spatial thinking** involves perceiving, explaining, and representing visual information. Spatial thinkers also mentally manipulate objects within space.

Visual/spatial thinkers use detailed **SPATIAL LANGUAGE** to describe the relationships between objects in space. This means using specific language of position, movement, and geometrical terms. Architects use content specific vocabulary to ensure the structures are correctly built.

Visual/spatial thinking involves **VISUALIZING** and examining structures using various **PERSPECTIVES**. Architects mentally manipulate visual information while thinking about how designs and shapes work together. Architects must view objects from multiple perspectives and varying viewpoints. Thinking this way allows architects to create aesthetically pleasing structures.

Visual/spatial thinking also involves **EXPLORING DIMENSION.** Dimension is the measurement of length in a direction. Architects draw up design plans called blueprints to show their ideas. Blueprints are flat 2-dimensional representations of the structure and can be measure in length and width. Once the building is constructed it will be 3-dimensional as it can be measured in length, width, and height.

Visual/spatial thinkers **SEEK STRUCTURE** or look for repetitions and patterns in order to organize visual information. For example, architects use graph paper to organize their blueprint drawings. They also have specific symbols for design elements such as doors and staircases. These structures are in place so that all architects can read from any blueprint.

In addition to visual/spatial reasoning, architects think creatively during the design phase and critically when analyzing and evaluating the information and making a reasonable decision. Being an architect requires various thinking strategies. Would you like to be an architect?

Handout I.2: Think Like a Disciplinarian
Visual-Spatial Thinking Like an Architect

Name: _____

What questions do architect ask?	What tools or thinking skills does an architect need?

Describe the main purpose of an architect.

Why are architects important in today's world?	How do architects think about new information?

❑ Model answering the questions on the Framing the Thinking of an Architect page (Handout I.2). Key understandings are outlined in Box I.1.

Box I.1: Framing the Thinking of an Architect: Key Understandings

❑ *What questions do architects ask?*
   ■ I wonder how they built that structure?
   ■ Is that structure safe?
   ■ What would happen if...?
   ■ How might I adapt this structure?
❑ *What tools or thinking skills does an architect need?*
   ■ Able to mentally manipulate objects in space.
   ■ Able to visualize.
   ■ Able to perceive, explain, and represent visual information.
   ■ Able to see things from a variety of perspectives.
   ■ Able to look for repetitions and patterns.
❑ *Why are architects important in today's world?*
   ■ Architects are necessary for designing and creating new structures.
   ■ Architects are important when developing aesthetically pleasing, functional, and safe structures.
❑ *How do architects think about new information?*
   ■ Architects read relevant books, articles, websites etc. to gather all information currently known about a topic.
   ■ Architects use the current research and trends to design new structures.
   ■ Architects look at past and presently used materials to see if they can use them in a different way.
❑ *Describe the main purpose of an architect.*
   ■ Architects enhance society by designing creative, aesthetically pleasing, functional, and safe buildings and structures.

❑ Tell students that throughout this unit they will be developing the skills of spatial language, visualizing, examining perspectives, exploring dimension, and seeking structure.

Primary Source: Artwork Analysis

❏ Display *A Sunday Afternoon on the Island of La Grande Jatte* by Georges Seurat. Allow students to carefully observe the whole painting. Then ask the following questions:
  ■ What is happening in the painting?
  ■ What are the people doing?
  ■ What activities are taking place?
❏ Distribute the Primary Source: Artwork Analysis page (Handout I.3). Read the introductory material with students, encouraging them to think about perspective, movement, and technique. Tell students that the art technique of using just dabs or dots of paint to create an image is called *pointillism*. Describe what you see in detail.
  ■ This is a painting of a park in Paris.
  ■ People are walking, lounging, and playing together.
  ■ We only see the sides of their faces.
❏ Guide students through answering each section on the page. Key understandings are outlined in Box I.2.

Box I.2: Primary Source: Artwork Analysis Key Understandings

❏ *Describe the technique used by the artist.*
  ■ The artwork was created using tiny dabs of differing colors of paint to create the images.
  ■ Seurat used varying shades of paint colors to show perspective.
  ■ The art technique of pointillism teaches the viewer that our eyes can be deceived and create an image of simple dots when the dots are structured accordingly.
❏ *How do our eyes* perceive *the painting? Why do we see it as we do?*
  ■ Our eyes see the juxtaposition of colorful dots as a whole, and our brain creates an image.
❏ *Do you think Seurat proved his theory? Why or why not?*
  ■ Seurat proved his theory that a painting created using only dabs of paint in differing colors would produce a brightly colored painting. He also proved that if he used tiny closely painted dots of various paint colors, this would allow the viewer's eye to blend the colors optically and create an image as seen in this piece.

Handout I.3: Artwork Analysis

A Sunday Afternoon on the Island of La Grande Jatte, Georges Seurat, 1884

Name: _____

Look at the painting by Georges Seurat entitled "A Sunday Afternoon on the Island of La Grande Jatte". This painting is interesting to visual-spatial thinkers for several reasons. One is the use of **perspective**. The level of depth and use of light both provide unique perspectives. This painting is also notable for its use of **movement, patterns, and shape/line placement**.

Another visual technique used by Seurat was **combining shapes**. It can be hard to see at first, but this painting is actually made up of millions of tiny dots to create the final image. This is especially remarkable considering the size of the painting: about seven feet tall and ten feet wide!

Seurat studied color and had a theory that a painting created using only dabs of paint in differing colors would produce a brighter colored painting than that of painting in strokes. He also thought that if he used tiny juxtaposed dots of various paint colors this would allow the viewer's eye to blend the colors optically and create an image.

See if you can see some of those visual elements for yourself!

Describe the artist's **technique**.

How do our eyes **perceive** the painting?
Why do we see it as we do?

Do you think Seurat proved his theory? Why or why not?

Handout I.4: Visual-Spatial Thinking Avatar

Name: _____

CREATE YOUR
VISUAL/SPATIAL THINKING
AVATAR.

DEVELOPING SPATIAL
LANGUAGE LIKE:

VISUALIZE LIKE:

CONSIDER PERSPECTIVES
LIKE:

EXPLORING DIMENSIONS
LIKE:

SEEKING STRUCTURE LIKE:

❏ Remind students they are using visual-spatial reasoning when analyzing this artwork.

Thinking Skills Avatar

❏ The final introductory lesson involves students creating their own "Visual-Spatial Thinking Avatar. Today, students will decorate their Avatar. Distribute Handout I.4.

❏ Discuss with students the concept of an avatar. An avatar is a symbolic representation of a person that can be used as a stand-in. As you move through the visual-spatial thinking sub-skills in this unit, this page will serve as a touch point for students to connect the skills together into one representation of visual-spatial thinking.

❏ Explain that throughout this unit they will be introduced to five learning targets:
   - Spatial Language
   - Visualizing
   - Visual Perspectives
   - Exploring Dimensions
   - Seeking Structure

❏ As students complete each target learning skill, they will pause and reflect on the key details of each sub-skill. Use the sub-skill boxes to record the keys ideas and/or illustrate a new avatar using the newly learned skill. This is a time for the students to synthesize their learning.

❏ Allow students time to illustrate their avatar (the outline in the top left box) to represent a visual-spatial thinking character/avatar of their choice. The other five boxes will remain empty for now, being filled in as students complete each sub-skill in the unit.

Bibliography

Kaplan, S. and Gould, B. (1995, 2003). *Depth & complexity icons, OERI, Javits project T.W.O. 2. Educator to educator. LVI.* J. Taylor Education, 2016.

Seurat, G. (1886). *A Sunday Afternoon on the Island of La Grande Jatte [painting].* Chicago, IL: Art Institute Chicago. https://www.artic.edu/artworks/27992/a-sunday-on-la-grande-jatte-1884.

CHAPTER 1

Sub-Skill 1

Spatial Language

TABLE 1.1
Spatial Language Sub-Skills Overview

Thinking Skill Outline	
Focus Questions	❏ How can we describe the positions of objects in space? ❏ How can we describe the movements of objects in space?
Lesson 1	*Language of Position* ❏ **Trade Book Focus:** *Henry's Map* by David Elliot ❏ **Practice Activity:** Spatial Language Scene Builders
Lesson 2	*Language of Movement* ❏ **Trade Book Focus:** *Slides, Flips, and Turns* by Claire Piddock ❏ **Practice Activity:** Slides, Flips, Turns Sort
Authentic Application Activity	*Reflections and Symmetry* ❏ **Trade Book Focus:** *Luka's Quilt* by Georgia Guback ❏ **Practice Activity:** Symmetry Quilts

DOI: 10.4324/9781003267942-2

Spatial Language Lesson 1: Language of Position

Objective: Develop the language of position.

Materials

- ❏ Handout 1.1: Spatial Language Anchor Chart (one enlarged copy for the class)
- ❏ Figure 1.1: Cereal Boxes on Store Shelf (project using document camera)
  - ■ Also available for viewing online at: https://unsplash.com/photos/wkvKZR4e2OI
- ❏ *Henry's Map* by David Elliot (teacher's copy)
- ❏ Handout 1.2: Read Aloud Reflection Page (one per student)
- ❏ Handout 1.3.a: Setting the Scene: Campground (one per student)
- ❏ Handout 1.3.b: Setting the Scene: Castle (one per student)

Whole Group Introduction

- ❏ Tell students that today we will be learning about spatial language. Explain that we use spatial language to describe relationships between objects in space.
- ❏ Show the shelf image (Figure 1.1). Ask students to locate items based on position and think aloud about positional words used to place items. Some examples of possible questions are the following:
  - ■ What is directly below/above...?
  - ■ Where is _____ in relation to _____?
  - ■ Which cereal is to the left/right of...?
  - ■ What is on the very bottom/top?
- ❏ Discuss the relative locations of various objects on the shelf. How can spatial language help us describe positions of items we are referring to?

Read Aloud Activity

- ❏ Share the book *Henry's Map* by David Elliot. Tell students that today you will read a story using spatial language.
- ❏ Draw special attention to words that help us determine positions of items in space. Pause at various points to elicit other descriptions for the positions of items described in the book.

SPATIAL LANGUAGE

DESCRIBING RELATIONSHIPS BETWEEN OBJECTS IN SPACE

Figure 1.1 Cereal Boxes on a Store Shelf Cereal boxes on a shelf for students to use spatial language when describing position

Handout 1.2: Read Aloud Reflection
Henry's Map by David Elliot

Name: _____

| Give some examples of spatial language (language of position) from the book. | How does spatial language help Henry? How does it help us every day? |

Follow your teacher's directions to complete the picture.

❏ Distribute the Read Aloud Reflection page (Handout 1.2). Direct students to carefully consider and answer the questions on the top half. When students have finished, discuss responses as a whole group. Key understandings for the read aloud are outlined in Box 1.1.

Box 1.1: *Henry's Map* Key Understandings

❏ *Story summary*: A pig named Henry tries to make a map of the farm where he lives. He walks around the farm, drawing the major areas as well as the animals who live in each spot.

❏ *Spatial language in the book*: Henry lives *next to* his sty. The sheep live *beside* the woodshed.

❏ *How spatial language helps Henry*: Spatial language allows Henry to locate animals and landmarks on his map. Spatial language can also help us find things and keep objects organized.

❏ Next, direct students to the bottom half of the page. Explain that they will be completing a directed drawing. You will read directions for the directed drawing exercise, allowing students time to complete each step.

1. At the bottom of your drawing space, draw a square that's about two inches long on each side.
2. Starting from the top left corner of the square, draw a horizontal line about two inches long. Do the same from the top right corner of the square.
3. Starting at the outer edges of the horizontal lines you just drew, connect each to the bottom corners of the square.
4. Erase the vertical lines from your square.
5. From the top center of your square, draw a vertical line that extends about four inches up.
6. Halfway up your vertical line, draw a horizontal line extending about two inches to the left.
7. From the far-left end of the horizontal line you just drew, create a diagonal line that connects to the top of your tallest vertical line.
8. Close to the top right corner of your drawing space, draw a circle.
9. Draw a short vertical line extending from the outer edge of the top center of your circle and an identical vertical line extending from the outer edge of the bottom center of your circle.

10. Draw a short horizontal line extending from the outer edge of the right center of your circle and an identical horizontal line extending from the outer edge of the left center of your circle.
11. Create four short diagonal lines extending out from the outer edges of your circle. Each of these diagonal lines should fall halfway between the horizontal and vertical lines made in the last two steps.

❑ Allow students to talk in pairs or small groups about the pictures they created. How did positional words help? What could have been clearer? Did we all draw the same thing? See Figure 1.2 for the image students should create through this directed drawing.

Figure 1.2 Directed Drawing Target Image

Skill Development Activity

❑ Now, students will work in pairs to complete a spatial language activity. This activity is similar to "Battleship," in that one player will set up a board and the other player will try and duplicate it without seeing the original image.

❑ Divide the class in half. Give each student in half "A" a copy of the campout scene (Handout 1.3.a). Give each student in half "B" a copy of the castle scene (Handout 1.3.b).

❑ Direct students to cut apart the five images at the bottom of their scene and glue them into place within their scene. When they finish, students should fold their scenes in half to keep them hidden from others.

❑ Pair students so that each team has one student from half "A" (campout scene) and one student from half "B" (castle scene).

❑ Distribute a fresh copy of each scene to each set of pairs. Students will take turns trying to direct their partner to recreate the scene they created by describing the placement of the five images at the bottom. For example, Player A will describe the placement of the cot, fire, log, duck, fishing pole, and cap to Player B using spatial language and without showing their original scene to their partner. Player B will attempt to place these items into their own scene using the clues from Player A.

❑ Teams will need to use specific spatial language to help their partner recreate their original scene as accurately as possible.

❑ Once Player B has completed the campout scene based on Player A's verbal description, the players swap roles, and Player A will try to recreate the castle scene as closely to Player B's original as possible.

❑ When teams are finished, have them compare their original scenes to the ones that their partners created based on their spatial descriptions.

❑ Discuss:
   ▪ How close were you to the original?
   ▪ What kinds of clues were most/least helpful?
   ▪ What do you wish your partner had shared?
   ▪ What can we learn from this activity?

Handout 1.3.a: Setting the Scene: Campground

Scene 1: Partner A will place objects, Partner B will try to re-create based on descriptions.

Handout 1.3.b: Setting the Scene: Castle

Scene 2: Partner B will place objects, Partner A will try to re-create based on descriptions.

Spatial Language Lesson 2:
Language of Movement

Objective: Develop the language of movement.

Materials

- ❏ *Slides, Flips, and Turns* by Claire Piddock (teacher's copy)
- ❏ Handout 1.4: Transformations Anchor Chart (one enlarged for the class)
- ❏ Handout 1.5: Slides Anchor Chart (one enlarged for the class)
- ❏ Handout 1.6: Flips Anchor Chart (one enlarged for the class)
- ❏ Handout 1.7: Turns anchor chart (one enlarged for the class)
- ❏ Handout 1.8: Read Aloud Reflection (one per student)
- ❏ Handout 1.9: Transformation Sort (one per student or partners)
- ❏ Optional: Transformations Dance Video:
    - ■ https://www.youtube.com/watch?v=sSsasVyYcdM

Whole Group Introduction

- ❏ Discuss the idea that spatial language can be used to explain position in space, but it can also be used to create movement.
- ❏ Show the students the transformation posters. Ask students if they have ever gone down a slide, seen a backflip, or changed direction in a line? These are all examples of transformations. Discuss each transformation and how they differ from one another.
- ❏ Explain that are going to play "Simon Says" using the movements *slides*, *flips*, and *turns*. You may need to model this by playing a few rounds together. The goal is not to see that last person standing, but to get the students to use their bodies to make a mind/body connection to the material.
    - ■ Have students stand and explain:
        - o The *slide* is a step to the right or left. (You will state left or right slide in the directions.)
        - o The *turn* will be a pivot on the right foot. (You will say "quarter turn," and the students will stomp with the right foot and pivot a quarter turn.)
        - o The *flip* will require students to jump and do a half-turn to face backward.
- ❏ Another option is to show the students the transformation dance using slides, flips, and turns. https://www.youtube.com/watch?v=sSsasVyYcdM

TRANSFORMATION

is a process which changes the position or orientations of a shape

FLIPS
(reflections)

TURNS
(rotations)

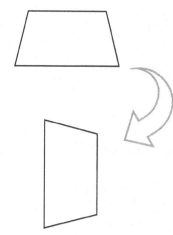

SLIDES
(translations)

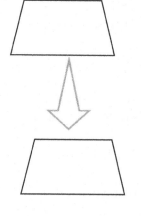

Handout 1.5: Slides Anchor Chart

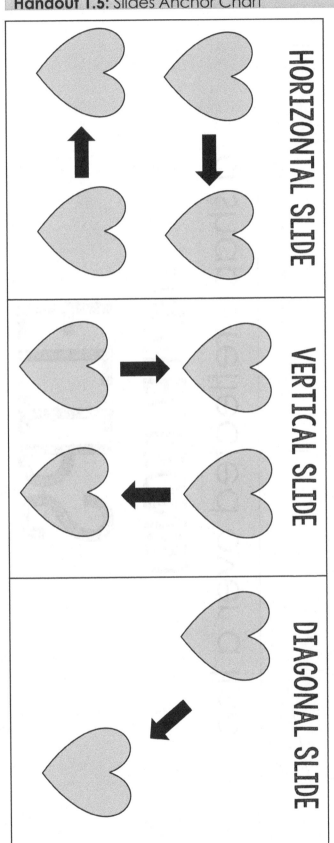

SLIDES
(TRANSLATIONS)
moves a shape in a straight line in any direction

HORIZONTAL SLIDE

VERTICAL SLIDE

DIAGONAL SLIDE

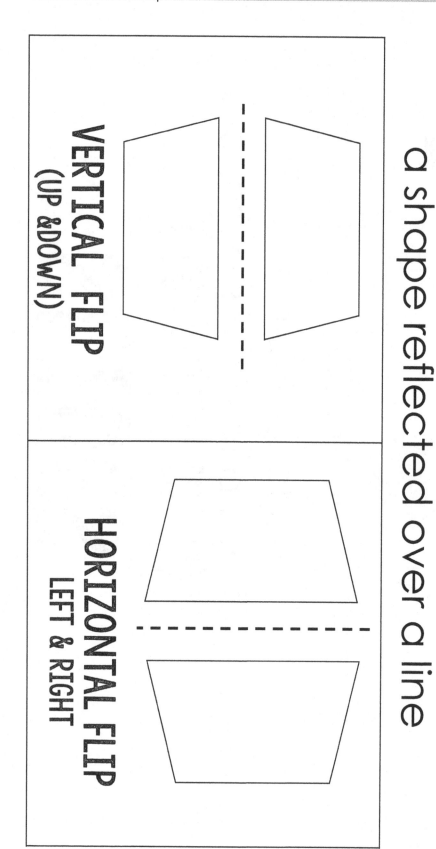

FLIPS
(REFLECTIONS)

a shape reflected over a line

VERTICAL FLIP
(UP &DOWN)

HORIZONTAL FLIP
LEFT & RIGHT

TURNS
(ROTATIONS)

a shape is turned around a point

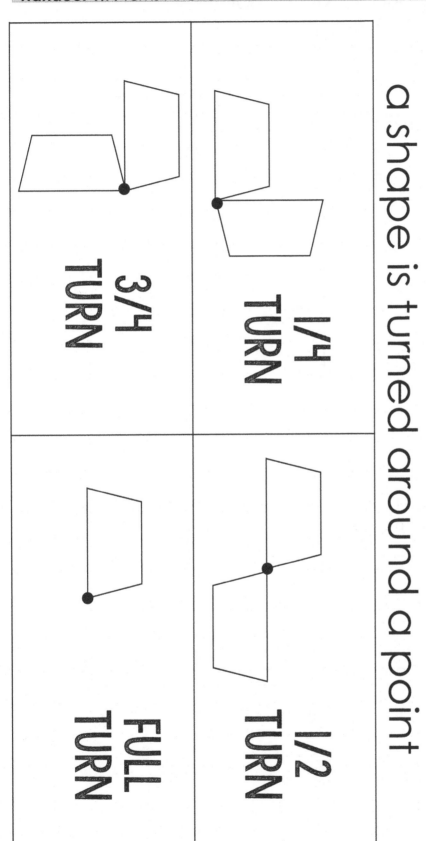

1/4 TURN	3/4 TURN
1/2 TURN	FULL TURN

Handout 1.8: Read Aloud Reflection

Slides, Flips, and Turns by Claire Piddock

Name: _____

Summarize the main idea of the story.	How did the book show spatial language?

Cut out the shapes at the bottom of the page. Follow the directions and glue each shape in the correct position.

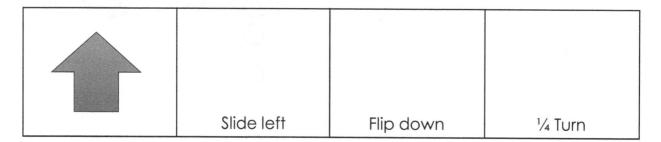

Read Aloud Activity

- ❏ Tell students that in this book, the main character will use transformations to create art.
- ❏ Read aloud *Slides, Flips, and Turns* by Claire Piddock. In this book, Sofia makes a special birthday card for her grandma by sliding, flipping, and turning shapes. Using the same simple steps, young children will learn about transformations as well as concepts such as *diagonal, horizontal,* and *vertical.*
- ❏ Complete the Read Aloud Reflection page (Handout 1.8). Allow students to talk in pairs or small groups to answer the questions. Key Understandings are outlined in Box 1.2.
- ❏ You may need to model the final question. The result should look like Figure 1.3.

Box 1.2: *Slides, Flips, and Turns* Key Understandings

- ❏ Sofia makes her grandma a card using transformations. As she learns about each transformation, she uses that on her card. She includes shapes sliding, flipping, and turning on her card.
- ❏ This book shows spatial language when teaching the different transformations. It also includes directional words such as *left, right, diagonal, up,* down, and *quarter turn.*

Skill Development Activity

- ❏ Distribute Transformation Sort (Handout 1.9). Tell students they are going to complete a transformation sort. The headings are at the top of the page. Students will cut the cards apart and sort them under the correct category.

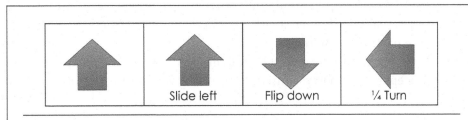

Figure 1.3 Handout 3.8 answer key

❑ Once students have completed the sort, have students glue the sort to another sheet of paper. You may use this as a formative assessment to determine who needs additional support in understanding the concept of transformations.

❑ Enrichment option: Have students create a card like Sofia did. Tell students to include at least one slide, flip, and turn on their card.

Spatial Language Authentic Application Activity: Reflections and Symmetry

Objective: Develop an understanding of symmetry in design.

Materials

❑ *Luka's Quilt* by Georgia Guback (teacher's copy)
❑ Handout 1.10: Read Aloud Reflection (one per student)
❑ Handout 1.11: Reflectional Symmetry (one per student)
❑ Handout 1.12: Rotational Symmetry (one per student)
❑ Handout 1.13: Classifying Symmetry (one per student)
❑ Handout 1.14: Creating a Symmetry Quilt (one per student)
❑ Handout 1.15: Quilt Square Patterns (one per student)
❑ Handout 1.16: My Symmetry Quilt (one per student)

Whole Group Introduction

❑ Tell students that today's lesson in spatial language will revolve around a special concept: symmetry.

❑ Pair students together and have pairs stand facing one another. Tell them that to start, we'll play a mirror game.

❑ Direct pairs to choose a leader for round 1. To play this game, the leader will move their hands in front of them (using broad gestures and moving somewhat slowly). Their partner will try to act as a mirror, following their movements. Remind students that while their feet can move up and down, their bodies should stay in one space. After a few minutes, have partners swap roles.

❑ After playing this game, tell students that this activity shows us the concept of symmetry: similarity between two halves of an object.

Handout 1.9: Transformation Sample Sort

SLIDE	FLIP	TURN

Read Aloud Reflection

❏ Tell students that we often see symmetry in artwork. One form of art-work where symmetry is often seen is in quilts.

❏ Read Aloud *Luka's Quilt* by Georgia Guback. In this book, a young girl and her grandmother make a traditional Hawaiian quilt. The book talks extensively about quilt design and showcases symmetrical quilts throughout. As you read, be sure to point out the symmetry you notice in quilt designs.

❏ At the end, discuss the following: How did symmetry make the quilts distinctive? How did it add to their beauty?

❏ Distribute the Read Aloud Reflection page (Handout 1.10). Direct students to carefully consider and answer the questions on the top half. When students have finished, discuss as a whole group. Students may add additional information to their answers after the discussion. Key understandings to target in the reflection are out-lined in Box 1.3.

❏ Direct students to the bottom half of the page. Explain that they are to create an image of a quilt similar to Luka's. Make sure to show sym-metry in your quilt.

Box 1.3: *Luka's Quilt* Key Understandings

❏ *Story summary*: Luka's family has a tradition of making quilts. When it comes time to make her quilt, Luka and her grandmother disagree about the design of the quilt.

❏ *Description of the quilts*: The quilts are divided into four quad-rants, each a repeat of the others. This gives the quilt both rota-tional and reflectional symmetry.

Skill Development: Authentic Application Activity

Teacher's note: There are many steps to this activity. Please follow the lead of your student population as to how quickly to complete each step.

❏ Distribute Reflectional Symmetry and Rotational Symmetry (Handouts 1.11 and 1.12). Together, work through the pages on Reflectional and Rotational Symmetry to build students' understanding of types

Handout 1.10: Read Aloud Reflection
Luka's Quilt by Georgia Gubak

Name: _____

Summarize the main idea of the story.	Using spatial language, describe the symmetry of the quilts.

Create an image of a quilt similar to Luka's. Be sure to show symmetry from one side of your quilt to the other.

Handout 1.11: Reflectional Symmetry

Reflectional symmetry is also sometimes called "mirror symmetry" or "line symmetry". For a shape to have reflectional symmetry, the shape must be able to be divided into halves by a line, with each half being identical. The dividing line is called the **line of symmetry** and can run in any direction: horizontal, vertical, or diagonal. A shape may have one line of symmetry, more than one line of symmetry, or may have no lines of symmetry at all.

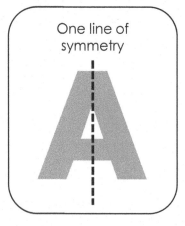

One line of symmetry

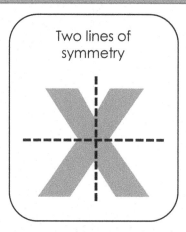

Two lines of symmetry

No lines of symmetry

For each of the shapes below, find the line(s) of symmetry and draw them. If there are no lines of symmetry for a particular shape, write "none" next to it.

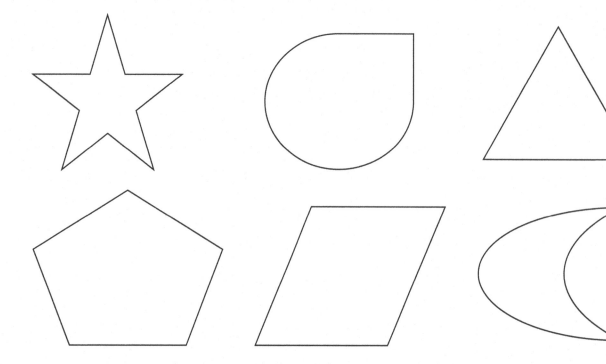

Handout 1.12: Rotational Symmetry

Rotational symmetry is when a shape looks the same after being rotated, or turned, around its center point by 360°. The number of times the rotated shape lines up with its original form is called the **order of rotational symmetry.** For example, if while rotating 360°, a shape exactly matches its original form twice (two times), it is said to have rotational symmetry with of order 2. If a shape only matches its original form at 360°, it is not considered to have rotational symmetry.

Original Position   Rotated 90°   Rotated 180°   Rotated 270°

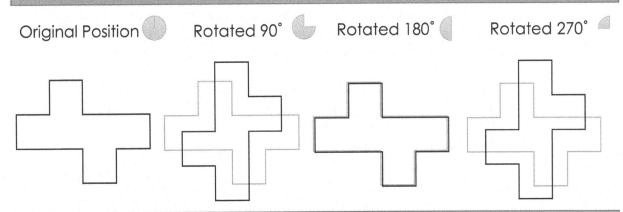

Look at this example. Notice how the shape changes position with each turn (the original shape is in gray underneath). The number of degrees refers to its rotation from the **original position.** One more turn would make 360°, returning the shape back to its original position. This shape aligns with its original form two times as it rotated (at 180° and again at 360°), so it has rotational symmetry of order 2.

Determine whether each shape below has rotational symmetry. If it does, tell what order.

Shape	Rotational Symmetry?	Order?
★		
(teardrop shape)		
(parallelogram)		
(triangle)		

of symmetry and the precise vocabulary used to describe it. Note: Rotational symmetry is a more complex concept, and students in younger grades may not have the mathematical schema to truly understand rotational degrees. Use your discretion and omit if needed. See Figures 1.4 and 1.5 for solutions to these handouts.

❏ Next, distribute Classifying Symmetry (Handout 1.13). Help students classify symmetry in classic quilt patterns using the classifying symmetry page. Solutions for this handout can be found in Figure 1.5.

❏ Distribute the Symmetry Quilt instruction, design, and template pages (Handouts 1.14, 1.15, and 1.16) to students. Provide students time and scaffolded support to work through these pages.

❏ Students will create as a final product a design for a symmetrical quilt. Encourage students to make these creative and colorful! Display student quilt patterns if possible.

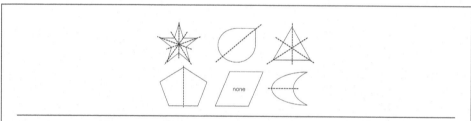

Figure 1.4 Reflectional Symmetry answer key

Shape	Rotational Symmetry?	Order?
★	YES	5
(teardrop)	NO	---
(parallelogram)	YES	2
(triangle)	YES	3

Figure 1.5 Rotational Symmetry answer key

Handout 1.13: Classifying Symmetry

Quilts are made to be useful, but also pleasing to the eye. In order to make them look nice, many quilters incorporate symmetry into their quilt designs. For each of the quilt designs below, determine how many lines of symmetry each has, as well as the order of rotational symmetry (remember, a shape/design that does not match its original design until it has been rotated 360° is of order 0.) As an added challenge, tell at what degree rotation each design matches its original form.

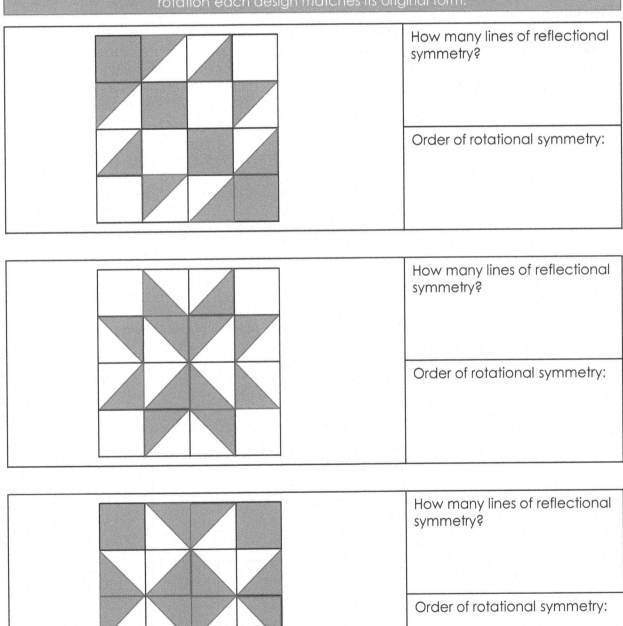

How many lines of reflectional symmetry?

Order of rotational symmetry:

How many lines of reflectional symmetry?

Order of rotational symmetry:

How many lines of reflectional symmetry?

Order of rotational symmetry:

Handout 1.14: Creating a Symmetry Quilt

Name: _____

In this project, you'll be using your knowledge of reflectional and rotational symmetry to create a symmetrical quilt design. When you finish, you'll have your symmetrical design on your completed quilt squares—a true work of art!

Steps:

1. Study the options for square patterns on the Quilt Square Patterns page. Think about how you'd like your quilt to look when it's done. Each square will become a 'half-square triangle' design, where halves of squares are shaded in triangular shape. Some squares may have no triangles shaded, and some may be completely shaded, but all shading can be completed with triangular shapes. These shapes will be laid out in such a way as to make your final, symmetrical design.

2. Using the Quilt Square Patterns page, sketch out a few options for how you could arrange your 16 quilt squares in a 4x4 array. Keep in mind that this quilt is meant to show symmetry! Consider:
    1. What lines of REFLECTIONAL symmetry can you incorporate? (Horizontal, diagonal, or vertical are all great options!)
    2. What degree of ROTATIONAL symmetry can you incorporate?
    3. Can you incorporate BOTH rotational AND reflectional symmetry?
    4. Is your quilt pleasing to look at, or does it appear random?

3. Your quilt must include at least ONE type of symmetry; for an extra challenge you may include more than one type of symmetry.

4. Decide on your final design for your quilt. Sketch it into the boxes below so that you have a plan for your pattern.

5. In each of your quilt squares, either shade (crayons or colored pencils work best) your squares or cut out triangles of colored construction paper and glue to each square to match the squares as you designed them. Remember that your shading should be in solid colors, but you can use any/all colors you'd like! Let your creativity shine. The order of your squares as you lay them out together should match your symmetrical design.

6. Create your final quilt design on the provided page. Be sure to make it colorful and symmetrical! Be creative and have fun!

My Quilt Design

Handout 1.15: Quilt Square Patterns

Name: _____

Each quilt square you create will be a traditional shaded fill in the form of either a solid or a half-square-triangle. You will use the shaded side to explore symmetry as you stitch your squares together into a quilt.

Choose a shaded fill for each of your quilt squares. On each square, you may either shade with crayon/colored pencils (markers are not recommended) or cut out construction paper triangles/squares to create the fill.

Possible Quilt Square Shading Fill Patterns

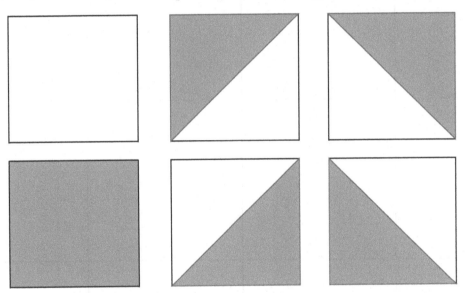

Using the six possible shading patterns above, create three different quilts using various shading patterns. See what designs you can make by shading each square with a pattern from the choices above.

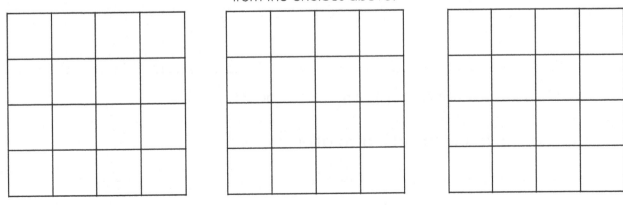

Handout 1.16: My Symmetry Quilt

Name: _____

My quilt has the following line(s) of reflectional symmetry:

My quilt has the following order of rotational symmetry:

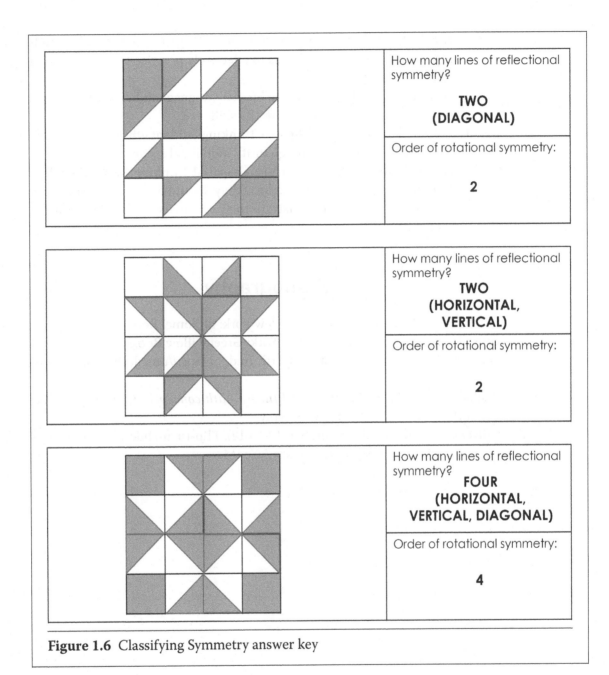

Figure 1.6 Classifying Symmetry answer key

Spatial Language Concluding Activities

❑ Conclude the chapter on spatial language with the Spatial Language Exit Ticket (Appendix A). Ask students to reflect on their learning about the skill of using spatial language to describe the relationships between objects in space. Allow time for students to complete the exit ticket. Use this as a formative assessment to gain a better understanding of your students' readiness to effectively practice the skill of using spatial language.

❏ If desired, complete the Group Spatial Language Rubric (Appendix A) to track students' progress with the skill.

❏ If desired, use the Visual-Spatial Thinking Student Observation Rubric (Appendix A) to assess and quantify individual students' mastery.

❏ Ask students to retrieve their Visual-Spatial Thinking Avatar (Handout I.3). In the Spatial Language box, they should either write the main ideas of this section or illustrate their avatar using the skill of using spatial language.

Bibliography

Elliot, D. (1952–2013). *Henry's map*. New York: Philomel Books.

Guback, G. (1994). *Luka's quilt*. New York: Greenwillow Books.

Photo by Franki Chamaki on Unsplash (n.d.). https://unsplash.com/photos/wkvKZR4e2OI.

Piddock, C. (2010). *Slides, flips, and turns, math concepts made simple*. New York: Crabtree Publishing Company.

University Academy KC. (February 12, 2012). Flip-turn-slide [video]. https://www.youtube.com/watch?v=sSsasVyYcdM.

CHAPTER 2

Sub-Skill 2

Visualizing

TABLE 2.1
Visualizing Sub-Skill Overview

Thinking Skill Outline	
Focus Questions	❏ How can we mentally manipulate visual information? ❏ How can we visualize shapes in our minds? ❏ How can we plan for movement of shapes (slides, flips, and turns)?
Lesson 1	*Mental Manipulation: Tangrams* ❏ **Trade Book Focus:** *The Warlord's Puzzle* by Virginia Walton Pilegard ❏ **Practice Activity:** Tangrams Puzzles
Lesson 2	*Mental Manipulation: Pentominoes* ❏ **Trade Book Focus:** Pentomino Party ❏ **Practice Activity:** Pentomino Puzzles
Authentic Application Activity	*Visual Puzzle-Palooza* ❏ **Trade Book Focus:** *Mouse Shapes* by Ellen Stoll Walsh ❏ **Practice Activity:** Visual Puzzle-Palooza

DOI: 10.4324/9781003267942-3

Visualizing Lesson 1: Mental Manipulation: Tangrams

Objective: Develop the ability to visualize and mentally manipulate visual information.

Materials

- ❏ Handout 2.1: Visualizing Anchor Chart (teacher's copy)
- ❏ *The Warlord's Puzzle* by Virginia Walton Pilegard (teacher's copy)
- ❏ Handout 2.2: Read Aloud Reflection (one per student)
- ❏ Scissors for each student
- ❏ Optional: Commercial tangrams sets for students
- ❏ Handout 2.3: Getting to Know the Tangrams (one per student)
- ❏ Handout 2.4.a–e: Tangrams Puzzlers (duplicated as needed and cut into half-sheet puzzles)
- ❏ Optional: Handout 2.5: Tangrams Math Extension (duplicate as needed)

Whole Group Introduction

- ❏ Tell students that now that we understand why spatial language is important, we need to be able to use that knowledge of position to move shapes. Great visual-spatial thinkers are able to picture these movements in their heads.
- ❏ Ask students to close their eyes and imagine the school playground. Ask several questions similar to the following, encouraging students to use their "mind's eye" to visualize this space. *Tailor questions to match the layout of your own space.*
  - ■ If I'm standing in front of the yellow tube slide, what is to my left?
  - ■ If I walk to the swings from the slide, what direction am I walking?
  - ■ What playground structure is to the left of the swings?

Read Aloud Activity

- ❏ Read aloud *The Warlord's Puzzle* by Virginia Walton Pilegard. This short story gives a great introduction to tangrams.
- ❏ Distribute Handout 2.2 (Read Aloud Reflection). Support students' understanding as they complete the Read Aloud Reflection page. Key

VISUALIZING

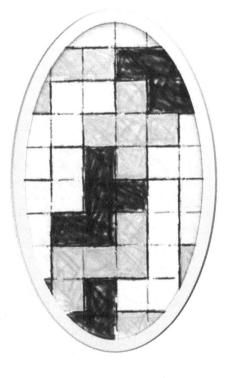

THINKING ABOUT HOW DESIGNS AND SHAPES WORK TOGETHER

Handout 2.2: Read Aloud Reflection

The Warlord's Puzzle by Virginia Walton Pilegard

Name: _____

| Summarize the main idea of the story. | How did the book show visualizing? |

Carefully cut out the square below. Then, follow your teacher's instructions to cut your own set of tangrams. Once you've completed your set, answer the questions.

How many tans are in the puzzle?

How many different shapes are there?

Which tans have a congruent partner?

Which two tans are different from the other five?

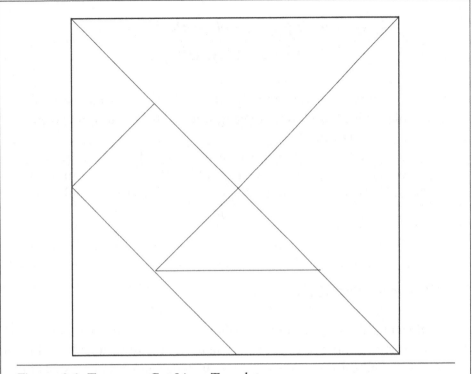

Figure 2.1 Tangrams Cut Lines Template

understandings to target are outlined in Box 2.1. Students will need scissors to complete the bottom half. Directions to cut out your own set of tangrams from the large square are as follows. Remind students that they'll need to attend to precision in order for their tangrams to be accurate! See Figure 2.1 for a key to the cut lines for this section.

- Fold your square in half diagonally. Crease well, then unfold and cut along your crease line.
- Fold one of your half squares in half again. Crease well and then unfold and cut along the crease. Set aside your two large triangles.
- Fold the other half square in half as well. Crease well and then unfold.
- Fold the vertex along this fold down and to the center of the long edge of the triangle. Crease well, then unfold. Cut the triangle off along the crease. Set aside your medium triangle.
- Cut the remaining trapezoid along the existing crease line.
- Fold one of your new trapezoids into a square and a small triangle. Cut apart.
- Fold the other small trapezoid into a parallelogram and the other small triangle. Cut apart.

Box 2.1: *The Warlord's Puzzle*
Key Understandings

❏ *Story summary*: A warlord helps the emperor piece back together a broken piece of china, creating one of the world's oldest puzzles—the tangram.

❏ *Connection to visualizing*: The warlord must visualize how the pieces fit together into new and different shapes. He must use slides, flips, and turns to get the pieces to fit as they should.

Skill Development Activity

❏ If you have them available, distribute a set of commercial tangrams to each student. If not, printable versions are readily available online for free download, or students may use the tangram set they created during the Read Aloud Reflection (Handout 2.2).

❏ Beginning with Getting to Know the Tangrams (Handout 2.3), allow your students to experiment with the tangram puzzles. Help students to get to know the relationships between pieces, and encourage them to slide, flip, and turn pieces to achieve designs. There are many possible solutions to each question, so no answer key is provided for this exploratory activity.

❏ Reproduce Handout 2.4.a–e. Cut each handout in half so that each half-sheet shows only a single puzzle. You may choose to duplicate each puzzle for every student, or you may choose to create small-group or class sets, depending on your needs and student population.

❏ Distribute the Tangrams Puzzlers cards (Handout 2.4.a–e) to students. These increase in challenge level from 1 to 10. It is recommended that you consider giving students the autonomy to self-pace where appropriate. You may also choose to work through the first few puzzlers as a whole group, gradually releasing students to work on their own and supporting those students who need additional time getting used to visualizing these types of puzzles.

❏ For an additional challenge, students may complete the Tangram Math Extension page (Handout 2.5). Solutions for this extension can be found in Figure 2.2.

Handout 2.3: Get to Know the Tangrams

1. Each piece of the tangram puzzle is called a **tan.** Label the tans at the bottom of this page. Use their mathematical names: **square, parallelogram, small triangle, medium triangle, large triangle**.

2. The two small triangles will completely cover the shape to the right (the square tan). Which other tans will the two small triangles completely cover?

2. Can you use two congruent triangles to make a pentagon? A hexagon?

3. Create a trapezoid using three tans.

4. Create a square using four tans.

5. Combine the two small triangles with the tans below to transform them into new shapes. Remember that the tans should be laid flat without overlapping!
   - Turn the **square** into a triangle
   - Turn **one of the larger triangles** into a quadrilateral
   - Turn the **parallelogram** into a triangle

TANGRAM PUZZLER #1

Cover this shape using:
- 3 tans
- 4 tans
- 5 tans

TANGRAM PUZZLER #2

Use the same FOUR tans to cover each of these shapes.

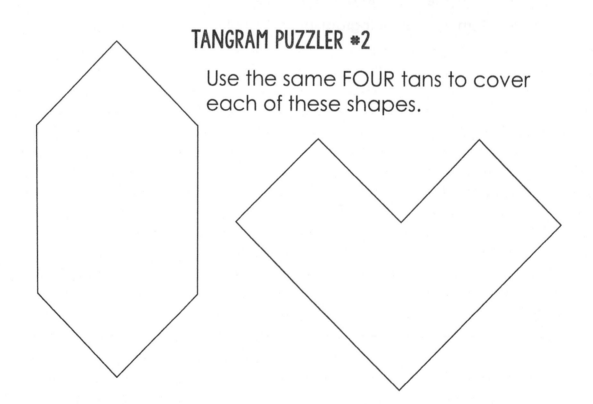

TANGRAM PUZZLER #3

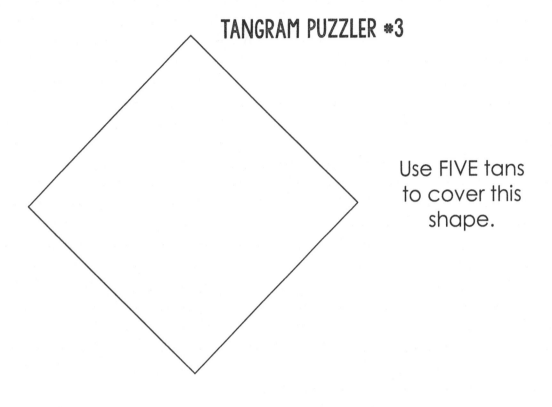

Use FIVE tans to cover this shape.

TANGRAM PUZZLER #4

Use FIVE tans to cover this shape.

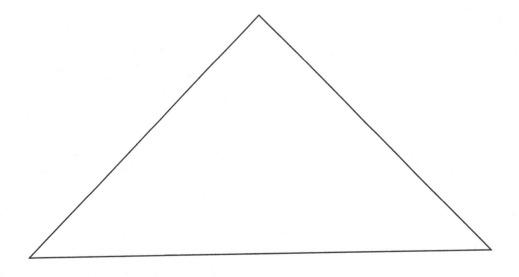

TANGRAM PUZZLER #5

Use all seven tans to cover this shape.

- -

TANGRAM PUZZLER #6

Use all seven tans to cover this shape.

TANGRAM PUZZLER #7

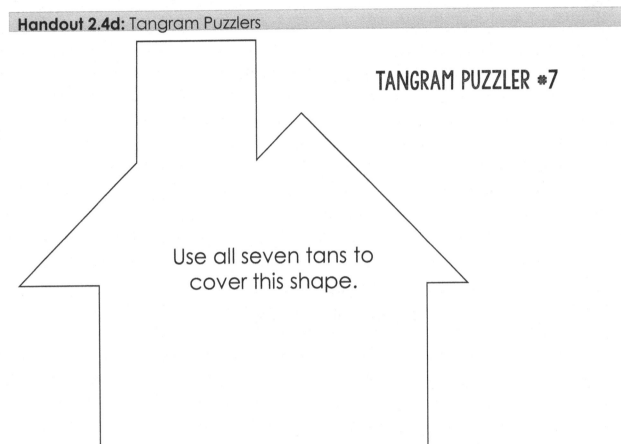

Use all seven tans to cover this shape.

TANGRAM PUZZLER #8

Use all seven tans to cover this shape.

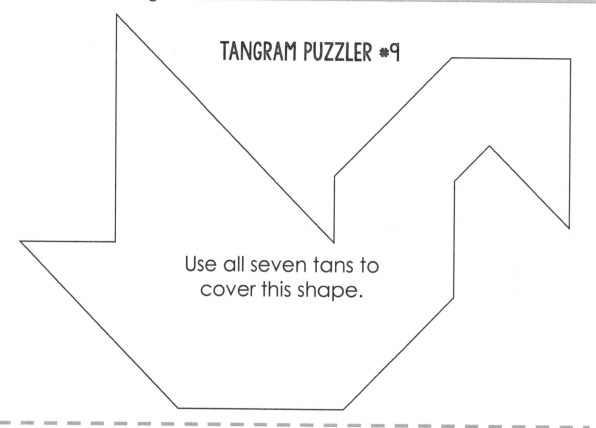

TANGRAM PUZZLER #9

Use all seven tans to cover this shape.

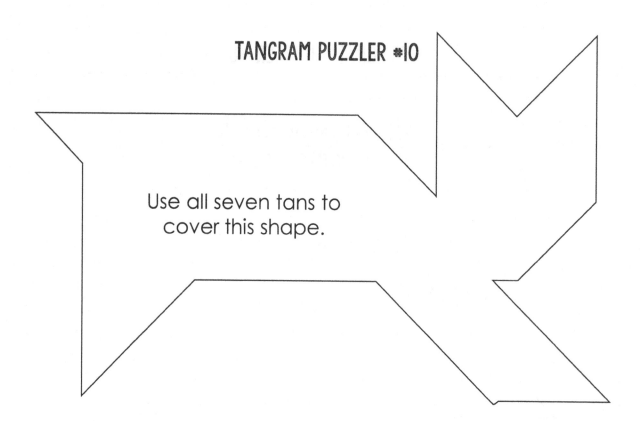

TANGRAM PUZZLER #10

Use all seven tans to cover this shape.

Handout 2.5: Tangram Math Extension

1. Look at the three large triangles. On one, place the parallelogram, on another the square, and on another the medium triangle. What other tans are needed to completely cover each square?

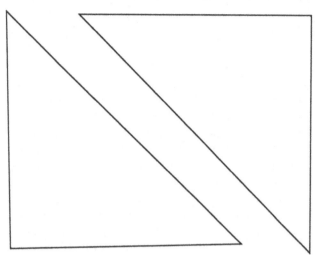 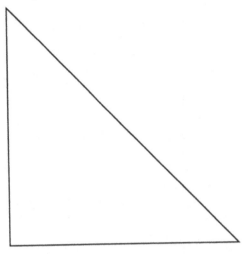

2. What does this tell you about the areas of the parallelogram, square, and medium triangle?

3. What fraction of the whole square Tangram puzzle is:
   - One small triangle?
   - One large triangle?
   - The parallelogram?

   Think: would this fraction apply to any other tans? Which one(s)?

4. Use the two small triangles to create:
   - A square
   - A larger triangle
   - A parallelogram

   What does this tell you about the area of the small triangle when compared with the areas of the medium triangle, square, and parallelogram?

5. If one small triangle is considered one unit of area, how many units is the whole 7-piece tangram square puzzle?

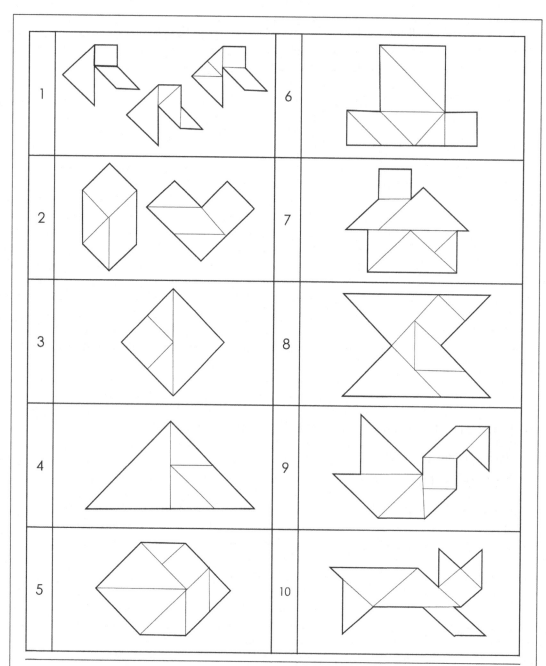

Figure 2.2 Tangram Puzzle Answer Key

1. Look at the three large congruent triangles. On one, place the parallelogram, on another the square, and on another the medium triangle. What other tans are needed to completely cover each square?

    You need the two small triangles to cover the remaining space in each triangle.

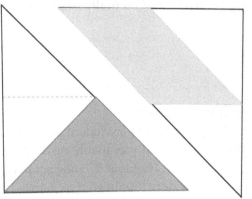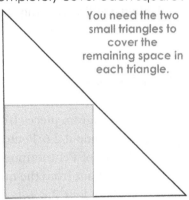

2. What does this tell you about the areas of the parallelogram, square, and medium triangle?

    They have the same area.

3. What fraction of the whole square Tangram puzzle is:

    *   One small triangle?   1/16
    *   One large triangle?   ¼
    *   The parallelogram?   1/8

    Think: would this fraction apply to any other tans? Which one(s)?
    Yes, the square and the medium triangle

4. Use the two small triangles to create:

    *   A square
    *   A larger triangle
    *   A parallelogram

    What does this tell you about the area of the small triangle when compared with the areas of the medium triangle, square, and parallelogram? The small triangle has an area equal to half of these other tans.

5. If one small triangle is considered one unit of area, how many units is the whole 7-piece tangram square puzzle? 16 units

Figure 2.3 Tangram Math Extension Answer Key

Visualizing Lesson 2: Mental Manipulations: Pentominoes

Objective: Practice the skill of visualizing and mentally manipulating visual information.

Materials

- ❏ Tangram pieces from the previous lesson
- ❏ Handout 2.6: Pentomino Party story (one per student or teacher's copy)
- ❏ Set of Pentominoes (either commercially available or duplicated and cut out from the masters provided in Handout 2.7; one set per student)
- ❏ Handout 2.8.a–f: Pentomino Puzzlers (duplicated as needed and cut into half-sheet puzzles)
- ❏ Optional: Handout 2.9: Pentominoes Math Extension (duplicated as needed)

Whole Group Introduction

- ❏ Give students a few minutes with the tangrams from the last lesson to create and share their own designs. Elicit discussion about how students used visualization to create their designs, including discussion of spatial movements (slides, flips, turns).
- ❏ Tell students that today they'll be experimenting with a similar type of spatial puzzle called Pentominoes.

Read Aloud Activity

- ❏ Read together The Pentomino Party (Handout 2.6) with students. Pause as each new pentomino piece is revealed to show that piece to students.
- ❏ If you have access to commercial pentomino pieces, show these pieces to students as you read. Alternately, you might distribute each piece to each student as it is revealed in the story so that they may have a concrete manipulative to explore.
- ❏ On the final puzzle page in the story, ensure that each student has a full set of pentominoes to experiment with (either commercial pentominoes or printed from the set provided in Handout 2.7). Encourage students to work alongside the story characters to fill in the final rectangle puzzle by placing the pieces in their corresponding spaces.

Handout 2.6: The Pentomino Party

Name: _____

Martha was struggling to concentrate on her homework. Math was her favorite subject, yet she couldn't finish these last few problems. Martha's mind was elsewhere. She was trying to come up with the best birthday party theme ever. This was an especially cool birthday because on the **twelfth** day of the **fifth** month she was going to turn **twelve**. This was her GOLDEN birthday, and she was determined to make it extra special.

She decided to take a break from homework and work on party planning. After searching many websites, she still didn't have any answers. Movie party seemed too bland. A unicorn party was too juvenile. That's when it hit her, her birthdate numbers gave her the perfect theme: a mystery party. This will be a surprise everyone will love!

YOU'RE INVITED!
On the 12th day
of the 5th month,
Martha will be turning 12.
Please join us for a
birthday mystery surprise.
Come to my house on
5/12 at 5pm.

The invitations were sent to her twelve best friends. Now it was time to put the plan into action. With that, she began developing the clues. She couldn't wait to share them with her friends!

Finally, the big day arrived, and all twelve friends arrived with mischievous smiles. Martha announced the mystery game would begin. She instructed the friends to gather round. Each friend would receive their very own clue, but it was up to the group to work together to solve the Golden Birthday Game.

With that the children's eyes sparkled with delight. The first card was handed to Vaughn who was so excited to have the first turn. He read the clue aloud for all to hear and quickly got an idea of exactly where to look! "Follow me, everyone!" he shouted and took off at a trot toward the entryway.

Vaughn
We need someone to
start the race,
You'll find the first clue
in a flowery place!

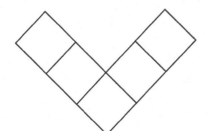

Off the children ran to the foyer front table and there in the center was a vase filled with roses. Under the vase was a strangle little shape. Vaughn picked it up and noticed something interesting. The shape looked like the first letter of his name!

Lily

In the next place you seek you might plug your nose, its hiding in the place I wash my dirty clothes.

Martha was pleased, the first clue was solved, she asked Vaughn to keep the shape somewhere safe, as they'd need it to solve this mystery.

She handed the second clue to Lily. Lily read the clue to her friends, and they quickly decided the place they should run was the laundry room.

That's where they discovered the second mysterious shape. "Look at this," Lily cried, "The next shape looks like an L which begins my name!"

Under the shape was the next clue. It was for Ursula and read, "To get to this room you must pick up your feet. Climb the stairs to find this playful retreat."

They all wondered a moment before Tom exclaimed, "Upstairs there is a game room! It must be up there." They all ran together and under the couch cushion they found the next shape which looked just like a U.

Ursula

To get to this room you must pick up your feet. Climb the stairs to find this playful retreat.

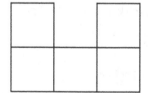

How funny this game was! The riddles, clues, and the hunting. The children all giggled; it seemed each kid would find their initial with a clue! Whose turn would be next?

Yamir's name was on the next clue, and his riddle seemed quite clear, grass is found outside, but where was the clue pointing exactly? There was grass everywhere! Then it hit them...the clue said they must not let down their "guard"... The grass they needed was in the backYARD!

In the center of the yard they saw a gnome statue with a clue taped to his foot. Another initial was soon clear... Y for Yamir!

Yamir

This is not time to let down your guard!
The next clue will be found near the grass in the ____.

Handout 2.6: The Pentomino Party, continued

Wanda

You're starting to get a feel for this game! Now look in the place we keep your pictures in frames.

Wanda read her clue with a gleam in her eye. She knew just where this clue would be, on the birthday party wall framed for all to see.

Off to the living room they all scampered. The next shape and clue were taped on the wall in an empty space labeled this year's picture.

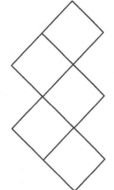

But Wanda was confused. Her shape didn't show her initial like all the rest. Tears came down her cheeks although she tried her best to be brave. Martha kindly suggested, "Why don't you try rotating your shape?" That did the trick, and now Wanda beamed as she saw the "W" clearly.

Next it was Tom's turn, and he was quick to figure out the next clue would be near the toy box.

Tom

Finding this next clue will be such a joy! Look for it where you'd put away a toy.

In the playroom they found the next shape and clue in the toy chest. There was no mistaking this "T"!

Philip was next. He was so excited, he read it too quickly and made a mistake. He ran to the kitchen, but there was no clue to be found!

Philip

You're on a roll, this is no time to slack! Your next clue is where you could pick out a snack.

His friends were confused as well until Martha pointed out there was one more room in the house that held food— and all of the snacks. "Oh, the pantry!" they exclaimed and moved to the left. Yes, the pantry held Philip's shape and the next clue too.

Zaine

You must keep your cool and not lose your head; Your next clue is at the top of the bed!

Zaine was worried his clue would be trickier than the rest. He thought there's no room in a house that starts with Z, what in the world could my clue be?

He read his clue and was disappointed to see his clue pointed to Martha's bed and that doesn't start with Z. Slowly, he walked to the bedroom to find, the Z-shape pinned to Ziggy the Zebra, Martha's favorite stuffed animal. Then he beamed with pride.

Nelly was the next to receive a clue. She looked all around and what did she see, but a weird looking shape taped to the night light. Turning it to the side, she could see the resemblance to a letter N!

Nelly

Look up and look down, look left and look right; the next clue is by something that helps me see at night.

Ivan and Fred received the next clue together. This was a two-part riddle solved with two initial letters.

Ivan & Fred

Working together you must feel so bold, Clues that you seek are in a place that's really cold.

This one is tough; we must figure it out. The coldest place in the house is the freezer and that starts with F, but what about Ivan? What could his be?

They raced to the freezer and on the outside was a shape labeled Fred and a clue on the back.

Fred was confused as he looked at his shape. How is this an F he thought? Martha reminded him this game is just for fun, think of the lower case "f" and bring the line all the way through. Ah yes, with a little imagination Fred could see his initial.

Handout 2.6: The Pentomino Party, continued

Now it was Ivan who too looked confused. "Where is my shape? Does the game end right here?"

Martha reminded, "Remember to use all the words in this clue. Where is the exact place we keep items cold?"

Carefully, Ivan opened the freezer, attached to the ice cream was the shape and the clue.

Xavier

How patient you've been! The last clue is yours. You'll see "X" marks the spot if you check the front door!

The kids all scurried toward the door with Xavier in the lead to find the twelfth shape and learn how to proceed.

When they got to the door, sure enough, they found one more puzzle piece. This one, it was easy to see, was clearly in the shape of an X. Xavier grinned widely and proudly held up the piece for all to see.

"Wait a minute! Along with each piece that we've found so far, we've gotten another clue, but now we all have our own pieces," commented Philip. Nodding in agreement, the children looked back toward the door where they found one final clue. Reading it quickly, the children whooped and ran toward their final riddle.

Well done, everyone! You've found all 12 clues!

Now on to the kitchen for the next thing to do.

If you solve the last riddle, a treat waits for you!

Then, Martha led them into the kitchen where they found a final clue. It looked like a board, but then when Wanda looked closer, she noticed something interesting: "I think my piece might fit right here!" she exclaimed. The others clambered to have a look. One by one, they realized that they each had a piece of this puzzle and all together, they made a beautiful rectangle!

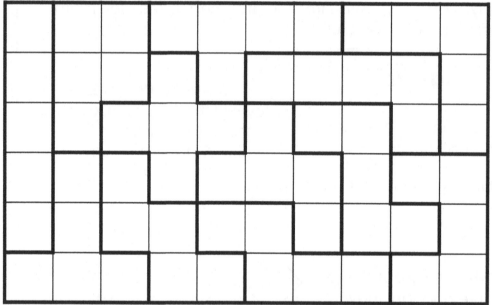

"Wow! Martha, that was a fun mystery, but I still don't understand your theme!" said Ursula. Martha asked her friends to study the shapes in the rectangle. Each guest looked at their own shape.

Then Nelly noticed something, "Hey, all of the letters are made up of 5 squares."

"Yes, and there are twelve total shapes!" exclaimed Zaine.

"Exactly!" stated Martha. "My birthday party theme is PENTOMINOES. Each pentomino piece consists of five squares that each share at least one side to create a unique tiled shape with an area of 5 square units. There are also twelve total pentominoes. This theme fits perfectly with my TWELVTH birthday on the TWELVTH day of the FIFTH month. Get it? A PENTOMINOES PARTY!" she exclaimed, as she added a candle decoration to the pentomino rectangle to make it a birthday cake.

All twelve friends were amazed at how clever the theme had been. Their excitement only grew as Martha brought out a tray of twelve tasty cupcakes, each decorated with...you guessed it... a pentomino piece! The friends all agreed that this was one of the best parties yet.

Handout 2.7: Pentomino Blackline Masters

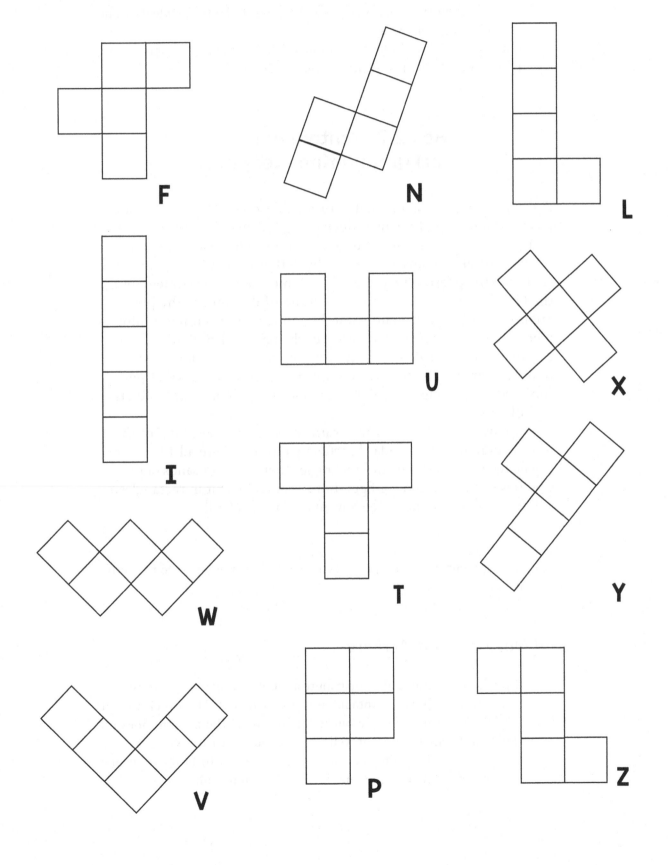

Scaffold supports as necessary, encouraging students to slide, flip, and turn pieces to achieve a fit.

❏ Once you have read the story, discuss the history and design of pentomino puzzles with students, outlined in Box 2.2.

Box 2.2: Pentominoes: Background Knowledge

Pentominoes are a mathematical tool that consists of 12 unique pieces. They were first introduced in 1953 by a mathematician and professor named Solomon G. Golomb. For ease of labeling, many mathematicians call them by letters which have similar shapes to the pentomino pieces. The name *pentomino* comes from the Greek *pente*, or five, and the -omino of domino, as the pieces are both mathematical and game-like in nature. Each pentomino piece consists of five squares that each share at least one side to create a unique tiled shape with an area of 5 square units. Many popular games have been based on the shape and nature of pentominoes, including the widely available and popular games Tetris and Blokus.

Pentominoes can be used in a variety of fun puzzles. One of the most common is the standard rectangle puzzle, where all 12 pieces can be tiled together to form a rectangle. There are thousands of possibilities for pentomino configurations that will result in rectangles, and it can be lots of fun to see how many one can find!

❏ Give students time to explore the pieces before moving on to the activity pages.

Skill Development Activity

❏ If you have them available, distribute a set of commercial pentominoes to each student. If not, printable versions are included here on Handout 2.7. Students can cut these out for themselves. The pentominoes on Handout 2.7 are sized to fit well with the puzzle cards. Note: If using commercial pentomino sets, students may need to build solutions beside cards, rather than using the cards as a template.

❏ Allow some time for your students to experiment with the pentomino puzzles. Help students to get to know the relationships between pieces, and encourage them to slide, flip, and turn pieces to achieve designs.

❏ Reproduce Handout 2.8.a–f. Cut each handout in half so that each half-sheet shows only a single puzzle. You may choose to duplicate each puzzle for every student, or you may choose to create small-group or class sets, depending on your needs and student population.

❏ Distribute the Pentomino Puzzlers cards to students (Handout 2.8.a–f). These increase in challenge level from 1 to 10. It is recommended that you consider giving students the autonomy to self-pace where appropriate. You may also choose to work through the first few puzzlers as a whole group, gradually releasing students to work on their own and supporting those students who need additional time getting used to visualizing these types of puzzles.

❏ For an additional challenge, students may complete the Pentomino Math Extension page (Handout 2.9). Solutions for this extension can be found in Figure 2.5.

Visualizing Authentic Application Activity: Visual Puzzle-Palooza

Objective: Apply the skills of visualization and mental manipulation.

Materials

❏ *Mouse Shapes* by Ellen Stoll Walsh (teacher's copy)
❏ Handout 2.10a: Pattern Block Blackline Masters (duplicate as needed)
❏ Handout 2.10b/c: Pattern Block Puzzles (duplicate as needed)
❏ Handout 2.11a: Block Design Cube Template (set of nine, duplicated as needed)
  ■ Alternately, these cubes can be created by shading the six faces of a blank-faced die cube, or these cubes may be commercially available.
❏ Handout 2.11b: Block Design Puzzles (duplicate as needed)
❏ Handout 2.12: Toothpick Puzzles (duplicate as needed)
❏ Handout 2.13a–d: Shadow Puzzles (duplicate as needed)
❏ Handout 2.14: Puzzle Reflections (one per student)
❏ Optional: commercial pattern blocks (class set to share)
❏ One-inch cubes, such as Unifix cubes or other similar blocks (class set to share)
❏ Toothpicks, preferably flat, not round (class set to share)

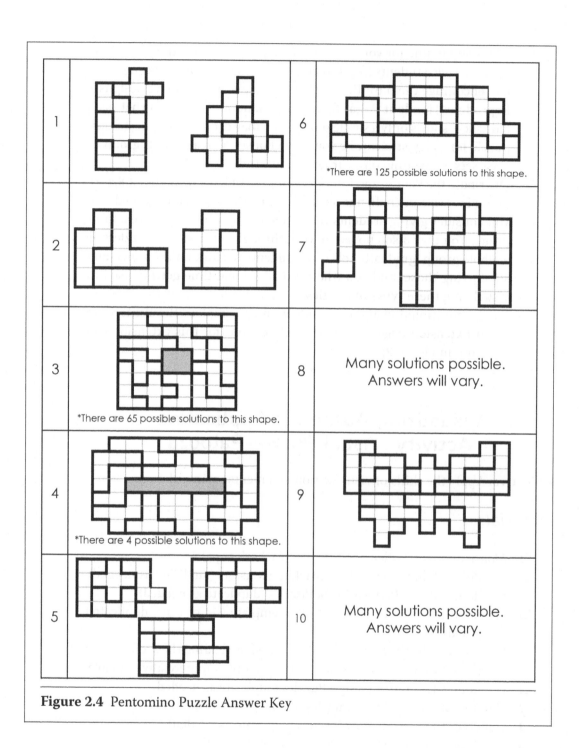

Figure 2.4 Pentomino Puzzle Answer Key

PENTOMINO PUZZLER #1

Use the same four pentominoes to fill both shapes. Which four did you use?

PENTOMINO PUZZLER #2

Use three pentominoes to fill each shape. You must use three different pentominoes in each (6 total pieces).

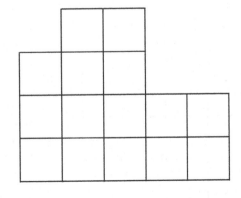

PENTOMINO PUZZLER #3

Use all 12 of your pentominoes to cover this figure:

PENTOMINO PUZZLER #4

Use all 12 of your pentominoes to cover this figure:

PENTOMINO PUZZLER #5

Fill this shape three separate times, using each of your 12 pieces only once. (Use different pieces each time you fill the shape.)

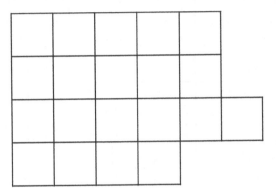

PENTOMINO PUZZLER #6

Use all 12 of your pentominoes to cover this figure:

PENTOMINO PUZZLER #7

Use all 12 of your pentominoes to cover the elephant.

PENTOMINO PUZZLER #8

How many words can you make using the letters in the pentomino set? Try to list at least a dozen words in which each pentomino is only used once.

Now, see if you can come up with ten more words if the pentominoes can be used more than once in the same word!

Handout 2.8e: Pentomino Puzzlers

PENTOMINO PUZZLER #9

Use all 12 of your pentominoes
to cover the butterfly.

PENTOMINO PUZZLER #10

Can you make all the letters of the alphabet using pentominoes?
Record your solutions on a grid to show which pieces were used to
make each letter.

*Hint: Don't forget that 12 letters are already made for you—they are
your original pentomino pieces!*

Sample: A

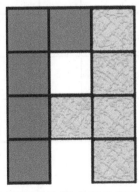

Handout 2.8f: Pentomino Puzzle Grid

Handout 2.9: Pentominoes Math Extension

Name: _____

Pentominos are a type of game piece that belong to a family of **polyominoes.** Polyominoes are made up of congruent squares joined at their sides, vertex to vertex. This family includes dominoes, triominoes, tetrominioes, and pentominoes among others. Each prefix (di-, tri-, tetra-, pent-) corresponds with the number of conjoined squares making up the pieces.

1. Think about how squares are joined to create polyominoes. Fill in the chart below to discover how many configurations of polyominoes are possible. Use grid paper to help you. Remember that flips or turns do not create new configurations!

Polyomino	Number of Joined Squares	Number of Possible Configurations
Dominoes		
Triominoes		
Tetrominoes		
Pentominoes		
Hexominoes		

2. Measure the perimeter of each pentomino. What interesting discovery did you make?

3. What are the possible multiplication arrays that would give a rectangle an area of 30 square units?

4. Try to build several different-sized rectangles with areas of 30-square-units using six of your pentominoes. Are all the arrays you named above possible? How do you know?

5. SUPER CHALLENGE: create an 8x8 square using all 12 pentominoes and one tetromino. Sketch your solution on a sheet of grid paper.

Pentominos are a type of game piece that belong to a family of **polyominoes.** Polyominoes are made up of congruent squares joined at their sides, vertex to vertex. This family includes dominoes, triominoes, tetrominioes, and pentominoes among others. Each prefix (di-, tri-, tetra-, pent-) corresponds with the number of conjoined squares making up the pieces.

1. Think about how squares are joined to create polyominoes. Fill in the chart below to discover how many configurations of polyominoes are possible. Use grid paper to help you. Remember that flips or turns do not create new configurations!

Polyomino	Number of Joined Squares	Number of Possible Configurations
Dominoes	2	1
Triominoes	3	2
Tetrominoes	4	5
Pentominoes	5	12
Hexominoes	6	35

2. Measure the perimeter of each pentomino. What interesting discovery did you make?

   All pentominoes have a perimeter of 12 units except the P piece, which has a perimeter of 10 units.

3. What are the possible multiplication arrays that would give a rectangle an area of 30 square units?

   1x30
   2x15
   3x10
   5x6

4. Try to build several different-sized rectangles with areas of 30-square-units using only **six** of your pentominoes. Are all the arrays you named above possible? How do you know?

   1x30 and 2x15 are not possible. There is only one pentomino piece with a width of 1, and not enough pieces with a width of 2 to make 30 square units.

5. SUPER CHALLENGE: create an 8x8 square using all 12 pentominoes and one tetromino. Sketch your solution on a sheet of grid paper.

   There are five possible solutions to this problem. The five tetromino pieces are:

Figure 2.5 Pentomino Math Extension Answer Key

Whole Group Introduction

❏ To start, work back through a pentomino or tangram puzzler as a group. Remind students that they should try to manipulate and "see" how the images will fit together in their minds as they work.

❏ Emphasize the critical point that mental arrangement of shapes means that students need to consider in their heads how shapes will fit together, and how they will slide, flip, and turn to create new images.

Read Aloud Activity

❏ Remind students that in both tangram and pentomino puzzles, simple shapes came together to form new objects.

❏ Read aloud *Mouse Shapes* by Ellen Stoll Walsh, pointing out how the mice use various shapes in combinations and new arrangements to create new images.

❏ Tell students that in today's puzzles, they'll also have to manipulate shapes to create new and unique images and arrangements.

Skill Development: Authentic Application

❏ For this activity, students will rotate through a series of visual-spatial puzzle "stations." Each station has a unique type of visual-spatial puzzle with four challenges for each type. Students can work at their own pace, or you can time stations to meet the needs of your students. If your students did not complete all the tangram and/or pentomino puzzlers, you might use the extra puzzlers as additional stations as well. Give groups of students time to work with each type of puzzle for several minutes, scaffolding support as necessary. After they've had time to interact with and solve some of the puzzles, have them stop, reset their materials for the next group, and fill in one section on their reflection page (Handout 2.14). Then, ask them to rotate to the next station to tackle a different type of puzzle. The puzzles for each station are as follows:

  ■ **Pattern Block Puzzles** (Handout 2.10): Using standard pattern blocks, students will cover the design areas according to the constraints on each puzzle card. These cards are scaffolded from least

Handout 2.10a: Pattern Block Blackline Masters

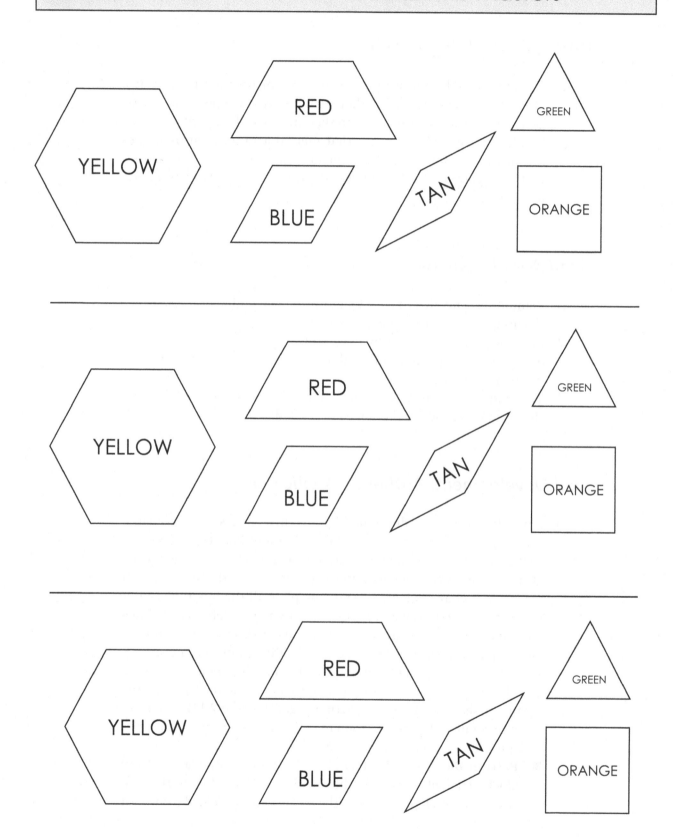

Handout 2.10b: Pattern Block Puzzles

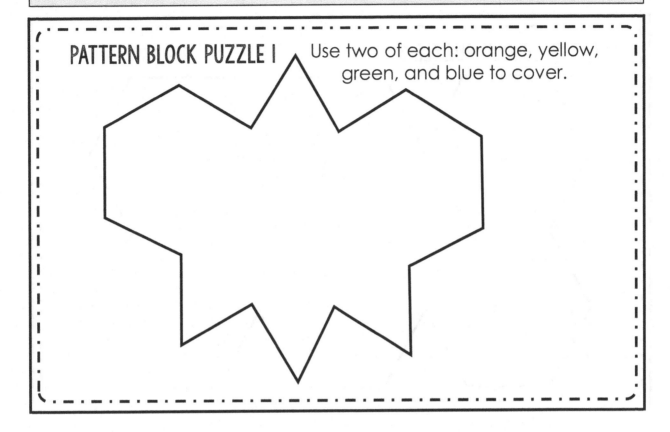

PATTERN BLOCK PUZZLE 1 Use two of each: orange, yellow, green, and blue to cover.

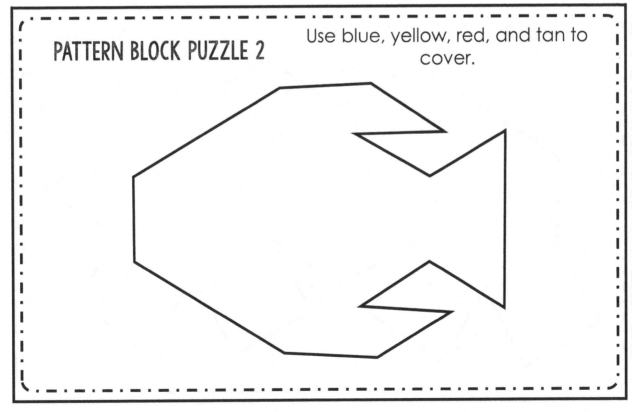

PATTERN BLOCK PUZZLE 2 Use blue, yellow, red, and tan to cover.

Handout 2.10c: Pattern Block Puzzles

PATTERN BLOCK PUZZLE 3   Use 14 blocks to cover.

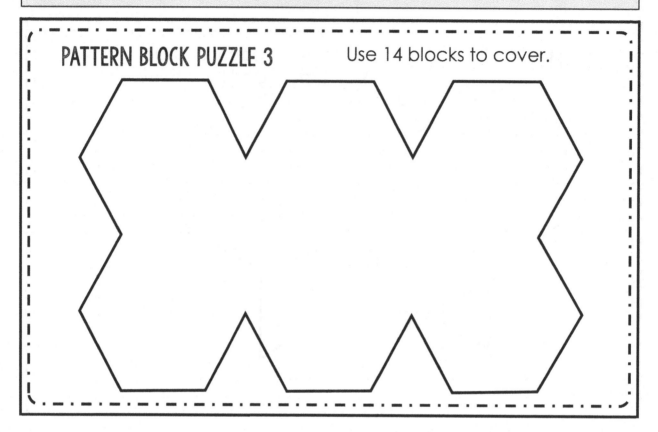

PATTERN BLOCK PUZZLE 4   Use between 15-20 blocks to cover.

abstract (puzzle 1) to most abstract (puzzle 4). Blackline masters are available in Handout 2.10a for duplication if you prefer students to have their own sets of blocks. See Figure 2.6 for sample solutions. Please note that these are suggestions only; many correct solutions are possible for these puzzles!

■ **Block Design Puzzles** (Handout 2.11): These puzzles ask students to use a set of nine shaded cubes to recreate a design. The designs presented on the cards can be made using a set of nine cubes shaded in half-square triangles. A cube net is provided for you, or you may choose to use blank die cubes and shade in the pattern shown on the net.

■ **Toothpick Puzzles** (Handout 2.12): Using a set of toothpicks, students will manipulate a design to achieve a goal. We highly recommend using flat toothpicks, as they don't roll off of tables/desks! See Figure 2.7 for solutions.

■ **Shadow Puzzles** (Handout 2.13): Each of these puzzles starts as a flat net which folds into a half-open cube. Students will use 1-inch cubes (like Unifix, volume, or linking cubes) to create a 3D structure that matches the figure's "shadow" as shaded on the net. Remind students that each side should be viewed from a "head on" perspective toward that side; for example, the bottom of the net should be viewed from a bird's-eye (directly above) view. See Figure 2.8 for solutions.

❏ Once students have had a chance to interact with all the puzzle types and have had time to reflect, discuss their reflections as a whole group. For key understandings to target, see Box 2.3.

Box 2.3: Visualizing Puzzles Key Understandings

❏ Students should recognize that they must mentally picture how shapes will fit together in order to form each puzzle's solution.
❏ Students should be getting more efficient in determining solutions for these types of puzzles.

Handout 2.11a: Block Design Cube Template

Print onto cardstock or firm paper. Fold on dotted lines and tape into a cube. You will need nine total cubes for the block design puzzles. Alternately, you could shade blank dice or cubes in the pattern shown below.

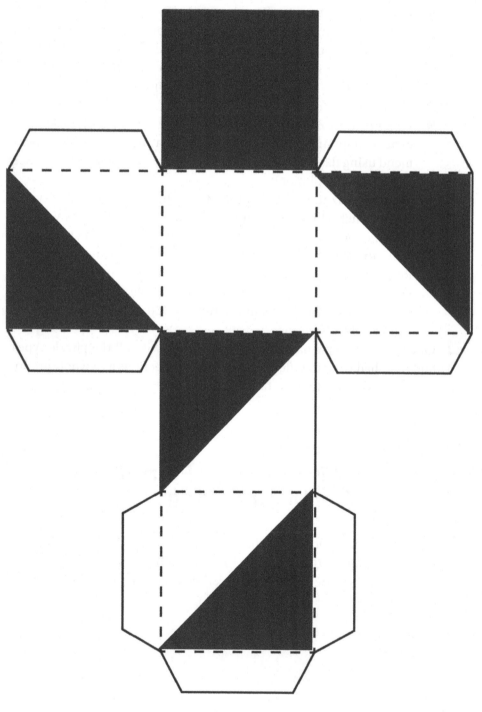

Handout 2.11b: Block Design Puzzles

BLOCK DESIGN PUZZLE 1

BLOCK DESIGN PUZZLE 2

BLOCK DESIGN PUZZLE 3

BLOCK DESIGN PUZZLE 4

Handout 2.12: Toothpick Puzzles

TOOTHPICK PUZZLE 1

Create the design shown below with your toothpicks.

Remove one toothpick to leave exactly three squares.

TOOTHPICK PUZZLE 2

Create the design shown below with your toothpicks.

Move only three sticks to make the fish appear to swim in the opposite direction.

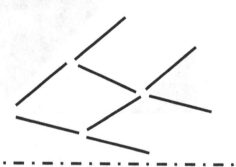

TOOTHPICK PUZZLE 3

Create the design shown below with your toothpicks.

Move two sticks to make exactly six squares.

TOOTHPICK PUZZLE 4

Create the design shown below with your toothpicks.

Move two sticks to make exactly four equilateral triangles.

Handout 2.13a: Shadow Puzzles

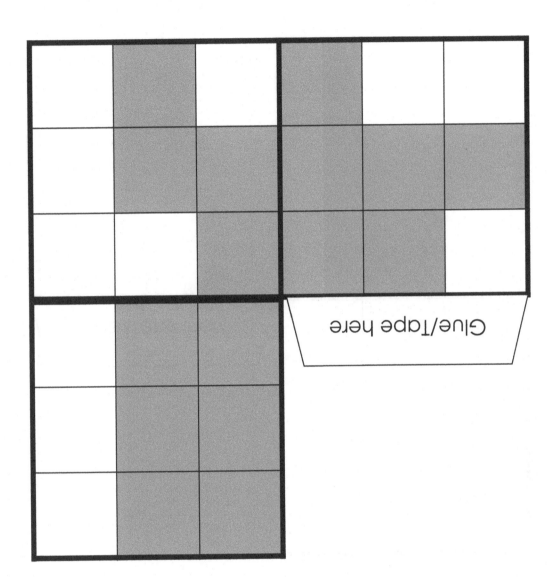

Glue/Tape here

SHADOW PUZZLE I

1. Cut around the outside edge of the net and fold inward to form a box which is open on three sides.
2. Use 1" cubes to build the 3D structure shown by the shadow in the net.

Handout 2.13b: Shadow Puzzles

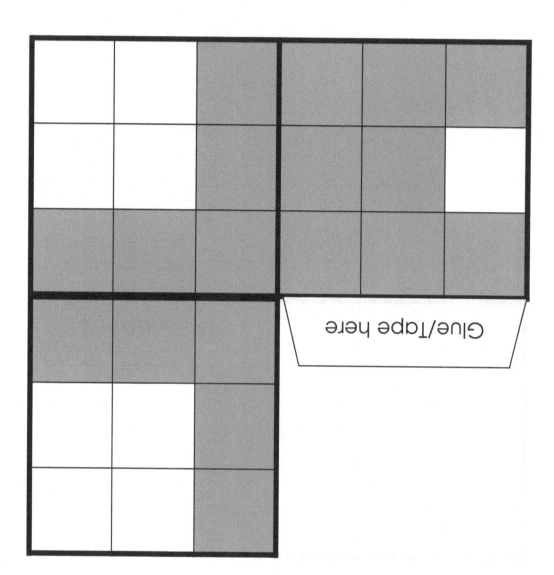

Glue/Tape here

SHADOW PUZZLE 2

1. Cut around the outside edge of the net and fold inward to form a box which is open on three sides.
2. Use 1" cubes to build the 3D structure shown by the shadow in the net.

Handout 2.13c: Shadow Puzzles

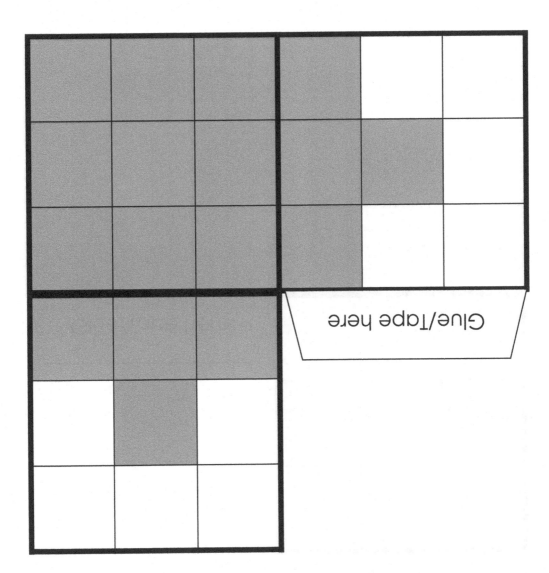

Glue/Tape here

SHADOW PUZZLE 3

1. Cut around the outside edge of the net and fold inward to form a box which is open on three sides.
2. Use 1" cubes to build the 3D structure shown by the shadow in the net.

Handout 2.13d: Shadow Puzzles

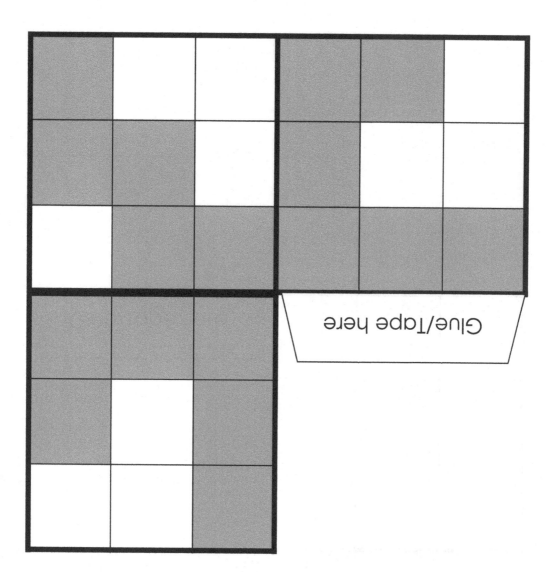

Glue/Tape here

SHADOW PUZZLE 4

1. Cut around the outside edge of the net and fold inward to form a box which is open on three sides.
2. Use 1" cubes to build the 3D structure shown by the shadow in the net.

Handout 2.14: Puzzle Reflections

Name: _____

Puzzle #1: _____ Describe the puzzle: On a scale of 1-10, how tricky was this puzzle? Why?	Puzzle #2: _____ Describe the puzzle: On a scale of 1-10, how tricky was this puzzle? Why?
Puzzle #3: _____ Describe the puzzle: On a scale of 1-10, how tricky was this puzzle? Why?	Puzzle #4: _____ Describe the puzzle: On a scale of 1-10, how tricky was this puzzle? Why?

My favorite puzzle was_____ because;

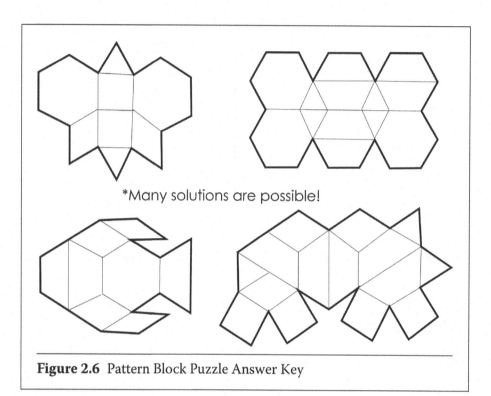

*Many solutions are possible!

Figure 2.6 Pattern Block Puzzle Answer Key

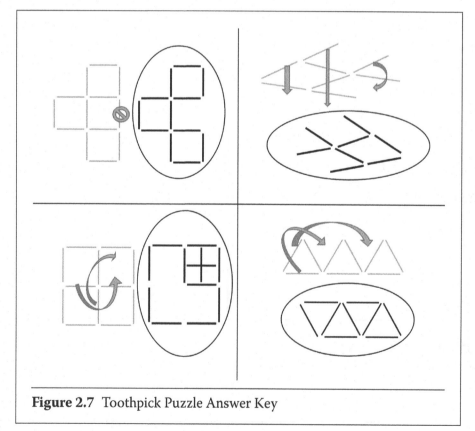

Figure 2.7 Toothpick Puzzle Answer Key

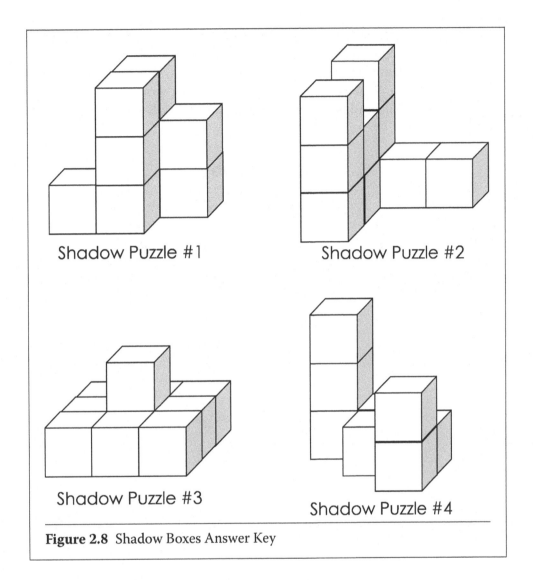

Shadow Puzzle #1

Shadow Puzzle #2

Shadow Puzzle #3

Shadow Puzzle #4

Figure 2.8 Shadow Boxes Answer Key

Visualizing Concluding Activities

❏ Conclude the chapter on Visualizing with the Visualizing Exit Ticket (Appendix A). Ask students to reflect on their learning about the skill of using visualizing shapes in order to mentally determine how they can move and work together. Allow time for students to complete the exit ticket. Use this as a formative assessment to gain a better understanding of your students' readiness to effectively practice the skill of using visualizing.

❏ If desired, complete the Group Visualizing Rubric (Appendix A) to track students' progress with the skill.

❏ If desired, use the Visual-Spatial Thinking Student Observation Rubric (Appendix A) to assess and quantify individual students' mastery.

❏ Ask students to retrieve their Visual-Spatial Thinking Avatar (Handout I.3). In the Visualizing box, they should either write the main ideas of this section or illustrate their avatar using the skill of using visualizing.

Bibliography

Golomb, S.W. (1994). *Pentominoes*. Princeton, NJ: Princeton University Press.

Pilegard, V.W. (2000). *The Warlord's Puzzle*. Gretna, LA: Pelican Publishing.

Stoll Walsh, E. (2007). *Mouse shapes*. Boston, MA: Harcourt.

CHAPTER 3

Sub-Skill 3

Visual Perspectives

TABLE 3.1
Visual Perspectives Sub-Skill Overview

Thinking Skill Outline	
Focus Questions	How can we represent information in visual formats? How are things seen from different perspectives?
Lesson 1	*Viewpoints*
	❏ **Trade Book Focus:** *Shrinking Mouse* by Pat Hutchins
	❏ **Practice Activity:** Moon Phases
Lesson 2	*Seen and Unseen*
	❏ **Trade Book Focus:** *Lucy in the City* by Judy Dillemuth
	❏ **Practice Activity:** Varying Viewpoints
Authentic Application Activity	*Illusions* **Authentic Application:** Questioning Perspectives **Application Activity:** Visual Illusions Booklet

DOI: 10.4324/9781003267942-4

Visual Perspectives Lesson 1: Viewpoints

Objective: Develop an understanding that our perception is dependent on our angle of viewing.

Materials

- ❏ Handout 3.1: Visual Perspectives Anchor Chart (teacher's copy)
- ❏ *Shrinking Mouse* by Pat Hutchins (teacher's copy)
- ❏ Styrofoam or other ball, preferably at least 8 inches in diameter (or combine two half-domes to create one sphere), painted half black and half white (one for display)
- ❏ Black construction paper (28 pieces)
- ❏ White chalk (one piece per student)

Whole Group Introduction

- ❏ Introduce the Visual Perspectives thinking anchor chart (Handout 3.1). Explain that one's visual perspective depends on examining the objects from multiple perspectives.
- ❏ Invite two students to come to the front of the room and stand back-to-back. Ask them to each describe the classroom as they can see it, without turning their head at all. *Do both students see the same things? Why not?*
- ❏ Discuss with students that our position affects what we see and how we see it. Considering our own visual perspective helps us to better organize visual information, as well as that of others.

Read Aloud Activity

- ❏ Tell students that in this book, a mouse seems to be shrinking. Tell students to be thinking about how the perspective is changing throughout the book.
- ❏ Read aloud *Shrinking Mouse* by Pat Hutchins. In this book, Fox, Rabbit, Squirrel, and Mouse watch their friend Owl fly off to a small wood in the distance. As he is flying away, Owl is shrinking. The group sets out to get him back before he shrinks entirely, but Mouse wonders as he chases after the others whether he is getting smaller, too. The group learns about visual perspectives through this "rescue mission."

VISUAL PERSPECTIVES

EXAMINING OBJECTS FROM MULTIPLE PERSPECTIVES

❏ Distribute and allow students time to complete the Read Aloud Reflection page (Handout 3.2). Think about how distance made perceptions different in the story. Conclude the reflection page by asking students to draw their school building from up close and far away. Go outside to get a good look at the front of the school building and gather this perspective if possible! Key understandings to target in the reflection are outlined in Box 3.1.

Box 3.1: *Shrinking Mouse*
Key Understandings

❏ *Story summary*: In this story, the animals begin to notice that objects in the distance look different depending on the angle and position of the viewer.
❏ *Connection to perspectives*: The way that objects are viewed depends on the position and angle of the viewer, as well as the distance from which they are viewed.

Skill Development Activity

❏ Prior to this lesson, you will need to get a Styrofoam sphere and paint (or duct tape) half of it black. This will be the prop for introducing the theory of visual perspective. Alternately, any ball or sphere can be used, and white and black duct tape can be used to cover each half of the ball.
❏ Tape or paint half of your ball black, and, if needed, paint or tape the other half white. Place the ball in the center of the room. Students will sit in a circle around the perimeter of the room. Each student will need one piece of white chalk and one piece of black construction paper. From their unique perspective, they will draw what they see. Students should really only be shading in the white parts of the circle from their vantage point, as the paper is black. Note that there are 28 days in a moon phase cycle; this activity can be done with fewer than 28 students/separate drawings, but in order to see a distinct progression, try to have at least 14 separate drawings, even if this means students complete multiple separate images.
❏ Give students each a clipboard, a piece of white chalk, and a sheet of black construction paper. Gather students in a large circle with the black and white sphere in the center. Ask students to sit down and draw the sphere from their perspective. Remind them that since the paper itself is black, they should not shade any black parts they see.

Handout 3.2: Read Aloud Reflection
Shrinking Mouse by Pat Hutchins

Name: _____

Summarize the main idea of the story.	How did the book show perspectives?

Picture the front of your school building. In the lenses of the glasses, draw a picture of the front of your school from a close-up (right in front of the doors) perspective as well as from far away (perhaps from the road as you approach the school).

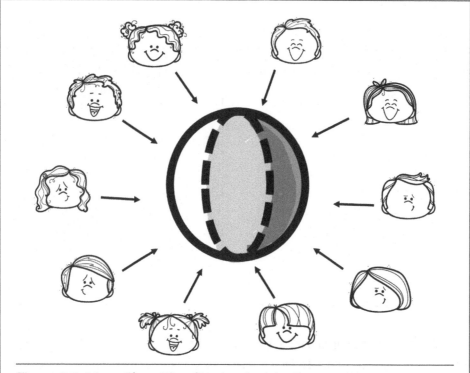

Figure 3.1 Moon Phase Visualization Activity Setup

❏ Post the pictures along the wall and ask students to observe the pictures. Ask students what they notice. Why are the pictures different when they were all looking at the same object? Share with them that this circular perspective also correlates to why we see the moon in phases in the night sky—we are seeing it from a different angle!

❏ As an optional additional schema-builder, show a video about moon phases, such as this example:

■ https://youtu.be/yXe0yxzYkjo

■ Conclude the lesson by asking students to summarize their learning based on the activities completed.

○ How does our position affect the way we see things? Why is this important to consider?

Visual Perspectives Lesson 2: Seen and Unseen

Objective: Practice the skill of examining shapes and structures from a variety of angles, thinking about parts which may remain unseen.

Materials

- ❏ *Lucy in the City* by Judy Dillemuth (teacher's copy)
- ❏ Technology to display a short video demonstrating visual perspectives:
  - ■ T-Rex Illusion: https://vimeo.com/82862051
- ❏ Handout 3.3: Read Aloud Reflection (one per student)
- ❏ Cube blocks (15 for each group of four students)
- ❏ Handout 3.4.a–c: Varying Viewpoints Cards (one set of cards—a, b, or c—for each group of four students, cut apart so that each student in each group receives only one card for their puzzle)
- ❏ Handout 3.5: Varying Viewpoints Reflection

Whole Group Introduction

- ❏ Ask students to recall their learning from the last lesson. What was interesting about visual perspectives? Why does the angle at which something is viewed matter?
- ❏ Tell students that they will now see a large-scale example of how visual perspectives matter. In this video, cardboard T-Rex dinosaurs appear to move, even though they are static (unmoving) the whole time. Begin the T-Rex Illusion video.
  - ■ T-Rex Illusion video: https://vimeo.com/82862051
- ❏ Pause the video at 1:30 to ask the students for any ideas about what makes the T-Rexes' heads "move."
- ❏ Finish the video, giving the students insight into how visual perspectives can change based on our viewpoint.

Read Aloud Activity

- ❏ Share with students that today's read aloud will deal with how visual perspectives can be helpful in real life. Read aloud from *Lucy in the City* by Judy Dillemuth, pausing to think aloud about how the owl's perspective is different from Lucy's, and why that would matter. How can seeing things from various angles help us?
- ❏ Distribute and allow students time to complete the read-aloud reflection page (Handout 3.3), asking students to draw a familiar object (their house, a school desk, a chair, or a piece of playground equipment, for example) from a straight-on perspective as well as from a bird's-eye view. How are these views similar or different? For key understandings to target, see Box 3.2.

Handout 3.3: Read Aloud Reflection

Lucy in the City by Judy Dillemuth

Name: _____

Summarize the main idea of the story.	How did the book show the importance visual perspectives?

Your teacher will give you an object to think about. Draw this object in the glasses lenses from two perspectives: looking straight at it from the front, and from a birds' eye view (above).

Straight Ahead

Birds' Eye View

Box 3.2: *Lucy in the City*
Key Understandings

❏ *Story summary*: When a small raccoon gets separated from her family in the center of a city, she can't seem to find her way back home. With help from an owl using his "bird's-eye view," Lucy is able to return home safely.

❏ *Connection to visual perspectives*: Lucy cannot find her way from her perspective on the ground. A bird's-eye view allows her to "see" how to find her way home, because of the difference in perspective.

Skill Development Activity

❏ Prior to this activity, prepare the Varying Viewpoints cards. Each page represents one design, shown from four unique perspectives. Cut apart these cards and paste each card to either construction paper or card stock (use a different color for each design to help you easily identify each of the different puzzles.) Fold the construction paper/cardstock in half to form a card (like a greeting card), so that students can easily stand up the card in front of them while they build. You'll need enough sets of cards so that each foursome has a single puzzle to work on (see Figure 3.2).

Figure 3.2 Varying Viewpoints Set-Up Directions 1. Directions to set up the varying viewpoint activity

Figure 3.3 Varying Viewpoints Set-Up Directions 2. Directions to set up the varying viewpoint activity

❏ Group students in teams of four. To each team, distribute one set of 15 blocks/cubes, and one set of viewpoint cards. Each student should take only one card for their puzzle. Students should sit facing each other with cubes in the center of their group, and each student should take one viewpoint card (see Figure 3.3).

❏ Students will each stand their viewpoint card up in front of them, without allowing any of their teammates to see their unique viewpoint. Then, foursomes should work together to build their block structures, verbally describing their unique perspectives and ideas based on their own viewpoint card. You may choose to have groups complete additional puzzles (see Figure 3.4).

❏ If students get stuck, encourage them to flip their cards upside-down for another viewpoint. Some other hints you may offer:

■ What can you see?

■ What might be unseen on your own card?

■ Which perspective are you seeing (Above? Side? Front? Back?)

❏ Complete this activity by discussing the questions on the reflection page. For key understandings, see Box 3.3.

Handout 3.4a: Varying Viewpoints #1

Cut apart the four cards. Each team member will get one card only, and they may not show it to the other group members. Working together, the team should build the block structure shown. Then, each member will hold their card at the angle it shows.

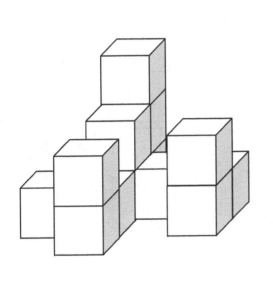

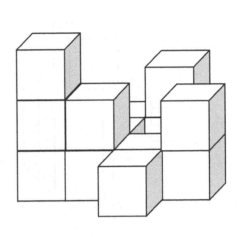

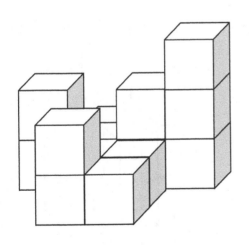

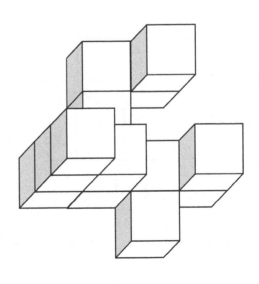

Various viewpoints of a structure 1

Handout 3.4b: Varying Viewpoints #2

Cut apart the four cards. Each team member will get one card only, and they may not show it to the other group members. Working together, the team should build the block structure shown. Then, each member will hold their card at the angle it shows.

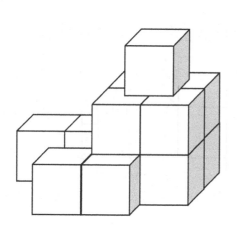

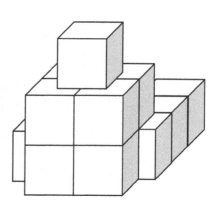

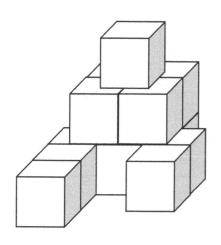

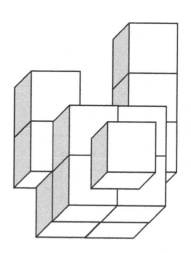

Handout 3.4c: Varying Viewpoints #4

Cut apart the four cards. Each team member will get one card only, and they may not show it to the other group members. Working together, the team should build the block structure shown. Then, each member will hold their card at the angle it shows.

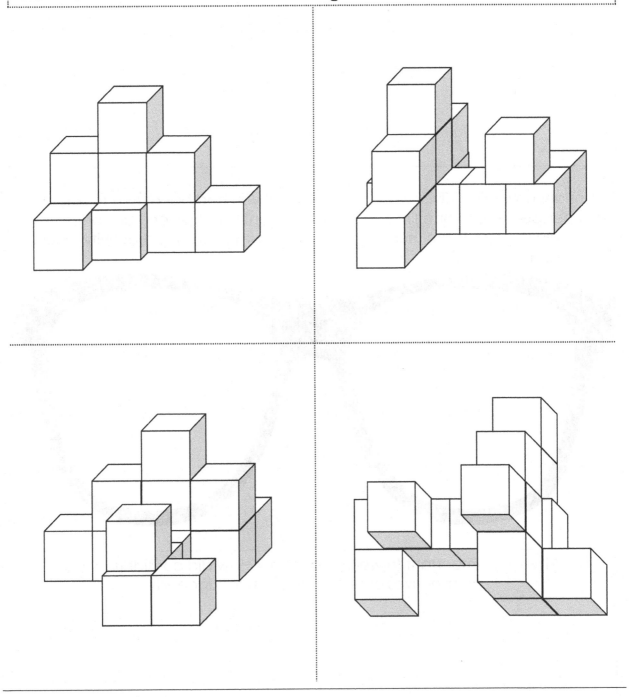

various viewpoints of a structure 3

Handout 3.5: Varying Viewpoints Reflection

Name: _____

Write a few sentences about the block building activity. What were your challenges? Successes?

Consider how this activity would have gone if you had been able to see all four perspectives at one time versus how it went with only one perspective available to each team member. Describe how you think the activity would have been different.

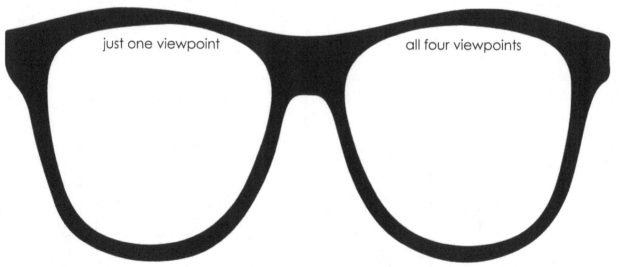

just one viewpoint

all four viewpoints

Why was it important to work as a team? How did considering the perspectives of others help you to succeed?

Figure 3.4 Varying Viewpoints Set-Up Directions 3. Directions to set up the varying viewpoint activity

Box 3.3: Varying Viewpoints
Key Understandings

❑ Students should recognize that no matter which one of the four viewpoints they personally worked with, there were blocks that were not able to be seen from a singular viewpoint. It was important for all four viewpoints to come together to gain a complete picture of each structure.
❑ Students should also be able to point out the importance of using precise spatial language (a skill from Sub-Skill 1: Spatial Language).

Visual Perspectives Authentic
Application Activity: Illusions

Objective: Apply the idea of visual perspectives to an authentic context.

Materials

❑ Projector or screen to show a short video from the National Institute of Health on Visual Perception

■ https://youtu.be/i3_n3Ibfn1c
❏ Handout 3.6: You Have to See It to Believe It! Booklet (one copy for each student, prepared according to directions)
❏ Six to eight toothpicks per student or pair

Whole Group Introduction

❏ Review the previous two activities with students. Ask leading questions to get them to think about visual perspectives:
  ■ Why didn't we all see the same thing when we were looking at the moon shape?
  ■ In "Varying Viewpoints," how did it help to know that there were parts you couldn't see?
  ■ How did you make sense of the visual information in the activity when you didn't know what parts you couldn't see?
❏ Remind students that when we're thinking about visual information that we must be sure to keep in mind that there may be more than meets the eye!

Skill Development: Authentic Application

❏ Today's activity will center around visual illusions and how the eyes work with the brain to take in visual information.
❏ Share this short video from the National Institutes of Health describing how the eyes and brain work together to process visual input.
  ■ Video Link: https://youtu.be/i3_n3Ibfn1c
❏ Prepare the You Have to See It to Believe It! Booklet (Handout 3.6) for each student.
  ■ Fold the front/back cover in half. The crease should be on the left side of the front cover.
  ■ Fold each of the inner pages in half with the text facing outward. The crease should be on the right side of the even-numbered pages.
  ■ Stack folded book pages so that even page numbers are stacked sequentially facing the top, starting with page 2.
  ■ Place the stack of folded interior pages inside of the folded cover page. Loose edges should be against the cover's fold, with the creased edge of the internal pages facing outward.
  ■ Staple along the left-hand side, using the provided staple lines as a guide.

YOU HAVE TO SEE IT TO BELIEVE IT!

TRICKS OF VISUAL PERCEPTION

Name:

HOW WE PERCEIVE VISUAL INFORMATION

When we make sense of the world around us using our sense of sight, we call this **visual perception**. While this is a physical process in our eyes, there are also brain-work involved. Our brains work quickly to make sense of the input coming in through our eyes.

Our eyes take in visual information. This information is filtered through the optical lens and retina, then through the optic nerve and into the visual cortex in the brain. In this way, our brain tells our eyes what we are seeing so that we can make sense of the information. This is called the **visual pathway**.

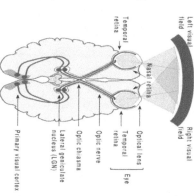

Because our brains are working so quickly to process new information all the time, we develop some shortcuts in perception. This means that often, our brains jump to conclusions based on patterns of knowledge and things we have seen before. Sometimes this means we need to look twice to make sure that perception matches reality!

Sometimes our brains jump to conclusions, which can lead us to see things that aren't there or miss things that are. When this happens, we call this an illusion. In this booklet, we will look at illusions to test our own visual pathways. We'll also create some neat visual art ourselves!

LITERAL ILLUSIONS

Literal illusions are images that *literally* are not what they appear to be. These images are made up of parts, and because of our brain's tendency to try and quickly make sense of visual input, what we perceive (see) and what is actually in the image are different. For this reason, we see something that isn't there!

In a literal illusion, our eyes are seeing the image quickly, and our brain is working to fill in the gaps without fully processing each individual aspect of the image. Once we consider these images more carefully, we are better able to see them for what they are—as the tricky sums of their parts!

RUBIN'S VASE

Look carefully at this illusion: what do you see?

Is there another way to look at this illusion? What else could you see?

ALL IS VANITY

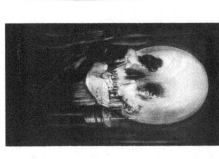

On first glance at this image, most people see a common figure. What do you see at first glance?

Look more closely: what is this picture really?

WOMAN'S FACE

The artist who first drew this image titled it "My Wife and My Mother-in-Law". Can you see both women's figures here?

Which did you see first?

4

PHYSIOLOGICAL ILLUSIONS

Physiological illusions are based on the limits of the physical eye. When we look at an image, our eyes are exposed to a stimulus, like color, shading, or placement of shapes. These stimuli activate sight receptors and in the case of physiological illusions, they overwhelm the receptors, causing us to perceive something that isn't actually there, like color or movement.

These illusions are different from literal illusions in that they don't rely on our brain's perception of an image. These illusions are truly tricks of the eye. For that reason, it's very hard to view them without seeing only the illusion!

HERMANN'S GRID

This illusion is created through our eyes' overexposure to stimulus (color). Look carefully at the grid. What do you notice at the intersections of the black squares?

When you stare directly at a single intersection, how does that change your perception?

5

PINNA'S RINGS

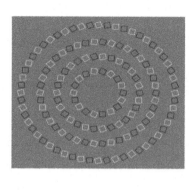

This illusion is one in which our brain incorrectly links images because of their placement relative to one another. Are the rings here linked? How is what you see different from what is real?

THE MUFFIN PANS

This illusion is one in which our eyes are tricked by crafty shading. Look at the muffin pan. Which compartments are raised vs. sunken?

Now, turn the image upside-down. Do the compartments change? How?

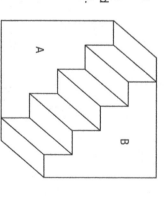

6

COGNITIVE ILLUSIONS

Cognitive illusions are fascinating because they don't trick the eye at all—they only trick the brain! These illusions are based upon our brain's tendency to make unconscious inferences (jump to conclusions). In these illusions, our brains struggle to make sense of images, and this leads to some interesting illusions where you have to draw your own conclusion about what you see (or don't)!

Cognitive illusions come in four main types: ambiguous (not clear), distortion (not level), paradox (non-sensical), and fantasy (not real). Fantasy illusions are also called hallucinations and are only ever seen by a single person. Each of the other types of cognitive illusion is discussed below.

AMBIGUOUS IMAGE: SCHROEDER'S STAIRS

Ambiguous illusions are those which can be viewed in different ways depending on perspective. Look at the image focusing on A and then again focusing on B.

How does the direction/depth of the stairs seem to change?

7

DISTORTION: CAFÉ WALL

Distortions are cognitive illusions in which our brain incorrectly perceives size, length, or curvature. Look at this famous illusion. Do the stripes seem horizontal? Check with a ruler: which is correct, the ruler or your perception?

PARADOX: THE IMPOSSIBLE TRIDENT

Paradox illusions are those which are technically impossible, but our brains struggle to make visual sense of. Look at the image of the impossible trident. What makes this image a paradox?

8

SORT IT: WHAT TYPE?

MÜLLER-LYER LINES

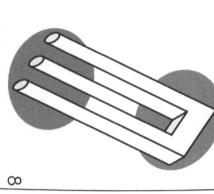

1. What makes this an illusion?
2. What kind of illusion is it?
3. How do you know?

DUCK OR RABBIT?

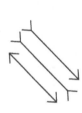

1. What makes this an illusion?
2. What kind of illusion is it?
3. How do you know?

PENROSE STAIRS

1. What makes this an illusion?
2. What kind of illusion is it?
3. How do you know?

KANIZSA TRIANGLE

1. What makes this an illusion?
2. What kind of illusion is it?
3. How do you know?

9

TRY IT WITH TOOTHPICKS

Your teacher will give you 6 toothpicks. Using these sticks only, try to make a single curved line. Draw your best effort here.

Is your curve perfect? What is challenging about this activity?

MARY EVEREST BOOLE

Mary Everest Boole was a self-taught mathematician and teacher who loved to find fun ways to practice math concepts with her students. She started her career as a librarian and wrote letters to famous mathematicians to learn more about math topics that interested her.

One of her most notable mathematics contributions was the idea of curve stitching, in which straight lines sewn onto cards formed parabolic curves. She found that when her students sewed curves onto small cards, they were able to better understand the number patterns, geometry concepts, and the underlying math found in design. Using Boole's method of curve stitching, you can practice these concepts in a fun way as well!

10

CURVE 'STITCHING'

Use a ruler to make sure that your lines are very straight!

Draw straight lines to connect the corresponding numbers on the x- and y-axis. The first line has been completed for you.

Continue drawing lines to connect each number, connecting 2 to 2 and 3 to 3, etc.

Using a colored pencil, trace the top intersections of the lines you drew.

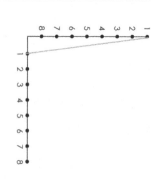

Look at the design you have created:

1. Did you draw any curved lines?

2. How does what you see (the completed figure) compare with what you know you drew?

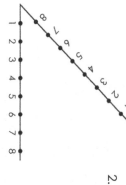

Repeat the process with the acute and obtuse angles.

11

CURVE 'STITCHING'

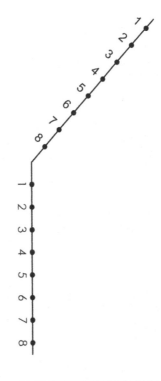

Now it's your turn! Label the x- and y- axes on this right angle with digits, starting at 1 on the top and the left. Then, connect the corresponding numbers using a ruler and straight lines.

How does this curve compare with the others you've drawn?

What generalization can you make about the relationship between the number of lines you draw and the illusion of a curve we create?

CURVE 'STITCHING'

The curves you created using straight lines are called parabolic curves. This means that the curves are symmetrical, rising and falling back at a constant rate.

1. Using your ruler, measure the length of each straight line you drew in the right angle. What do you notice?

2. Describe how starting with a right, acute, or obtuse angle affected the final design.

3. What does curve stitching show us about this type of curve?

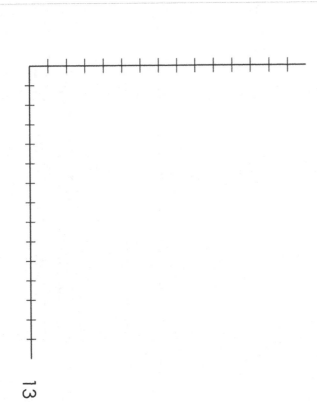

CURVE 'STITCHING' EXTENSION

What other designs can you make? What happens if you extend you design into four quadrants? Experiment to see what other designs you could make.

14

REFLECTION: WHAT CAN ILLUSIONS TEACH US ABOUT VISUAL PERSPECTIVES?

15

- ■ If desired, place a strip of tape along the left-hand side to cover the staples, trimming any excess.
- ❏ Distribute the You Have to See It to Believe It! Booklet (Handout 3.6) to each student. Scaffolding support as appropriate, work through the booklet with students (or allow students to work through the booklet with pairs or small groups). Give students time to explore, discover, and discuss the various images, illusions, and activities.
- ❏ When students come to the section on curve stitching (page 10 in the booklet), give them each 6–8 toothpicks to experiment with before moving on. As students experiment, engage them in questioning their perspective and how they're processing the visual information.
- ❏ Once students have completed the booklet, give the whole group time to reflect on the final reflection question. Give students about 5 minutes to complete a quick write, exploring their thinking and understanding of visual perspectives. Then, elicit responses from students to share their reactions.

Visual Perspectives Concluding Activities

- ❏ Conclude the chapter on Visual Perspectives with the Visual Perspectives Exit Ticket (Appendix A). Ask students to reflect on their learning about the skill of using Visual Perspectives, thinking about what is seen and what is unseen, and viewing things from a variety of angles and positions. Allow time for students to complete the exit ticket. Use this as a formative assessment to gain a better understanding of your students' readiness to effectively practice the skill of using Visual Perspectives.
- ❏ If desired, complete the Group Visual Perspectives Rubric (Appendix A) to track students' progress with the skill.
- ❏ If desired, use the Visual-Spatial Thinking Student Observation Rubric (Appendix A) to assess and quantify individual students' mastery.
- ❏ Ask students to retrieve their Visual-Spatial Thinking Avatar (Handout I.3). In the Visual Perspectives box, they should either write the main ideas of this section or illustrate their avatar using the skill of using visual perspectives.

Bibliography

Dillemuth, J. (2007). *Lucy in the city*. Magination Press, American Psychological Association.

Hutchins, P. (2000). *Shrinking mouse*. Scholastic.

Optical illusions and how they work. (n.d.). American Museum of Natural History. https://www.amnh.org/explore/ology/brain/optical-illusions-and -how-they-work.

T-Rex illusion video by Liquid Flame on Vimeo. (n.d.). https://vimeo.com /82862051.

The illusions index. (n.d.). https://www.illusionsindex.org/.

The visual system: How your eyes work by the National Eye Institute. (n.d.). NIH. https://youtu.be/i3_n3Ibfn1c.

Types of optical illusions, clear eyes. (n.d.). https://www.cleareyes.com/eye-care -blog/201610/types-optical-illusions.

CHAPTER 4

Sub-Skill 4

Exploring Dimensions

TABLE 4.1
Exploring Dimensions Sub-Skill Overview

Thinking Skill Outline	
Focus Questions	❏ How can we visualize and construct objects? ❏ What does it mean for an object to have dimension?
Lesson 1	*Building 3D Shapes* ❏ **Trade Book Focus:** *Iggy Peck, Architect* by Andrea Beatty ❏ **Practice Activity:** Using 2D blueprints to create 3D shapes
Lesson 2	*Comparing Dimensions* ❏ **Trade Book Focus:** *Mummy Math* by Cindy Neuschwander ❏ **Practice Activity:** Making nets/is this a net?
Authentic Application Activity	*The Math of Origami* ❏ **Trade Book Focus:** *More-igami* by Dori Kleber ❏ **Practice Activity:** The Four Rules of Origami

DOI: 10.4324/9781003267942-5

Exploring Dimensions Lesson 1: Building 3D Shapes

Objective: Learn about types of dimension and create 3D shapes from 2D shapes.

Materials

- ❏ Handout 4.1: Exploring Dimensions Anchor Chart (one enlarged copy for the class)
- ❏ Handout 4.2: Dimensions Anchor Chart (one enlarged copy for the class)
- ❏ *Iggy Peck, Architect* by Andrea Beatty (teacher's copy)
- ❏ Scratch Paper (at least one sheet per student)
- ❏ Handout 4.3: Read Aloud Reflection (one per student)
- ❏ Handout 4.4: Polyhedrons Anchor Chart (one enlarged copy for the class)
- ❏ Handout 4.5.a–b: Building 3D structures form 2D shapes (duplicate as needed on cardstock and cut apart so that each student has one structure to make)
- ❏ Handout 4.5: Building Abstract Polyhedrons (duplicate as needed; distribute cards to students who show readiness for a new challenge)
- ❏ Marshmallows
- ❏ Toothpicks
- ❏ Handout 4.6: Geometry Prefixes Anchor Chart (one enlarged copy for the class)

Whole Group Introduction

- ❏ Remind students that in the previous lessons they examined shapes and structures from a variety of perspectives. An artist can vary the perspective by drawing solid objects on a sheet of paper to give the right impression of the objects' length, depth, height, or position in relation to each other. This is called giving the impression of a three-dimensional (3D) solid on a two-dimensional (2D) surface.
- ❏ Ask students if they know what the word *dimension* means. Allow students time to generate ideas. Show the students the Exploring Dimensions Anchor Chart (Handout 4.1). Explain that in math, *dimension* is the measurement of length in one direction.

EXPLORING DIMENSIONS

VISUALIZING AND CONSTRUCTING OBJECTS

❏ Next display the Dimension Anchor Chart (Handout 4.2). Explain the difference between 0D, 1D, 2D, and 3D. Give each student a piece of scratch paper.

■ Have students point their pencils in the air, and tell them to visualize the point of space their pencil tip is touching. Ask students how to measure this point in space. Guide students in discovering that it can't be measured, making it an example of a 0D figure.

■ Next, have students draw a straight line on their piece of paper. Ask students how they would measure the line. Guide students in discovering it can be measured by length only, making it an example of a 1D figure.

■ Tell students to turn the line into a triangle, square, or rectangle. Ask students how they could measure the shape. Guide students in discovering that it can be measured in both height and width, making it an example of a 2D shape.

■ Finally, tell students to crumple their piece of paper into a ball. Ask students how they could measure the ball. Guide students in discovering that it can be measured in height, length, and width, making it an example of a 3D shape.

Read Aloud Activity

❏ Tell students that an architect is a person who designs plans for structures. They use their knowledge of dimension to create blueprints which are detailed 2D plans on how to build 3D structures.

❏ Read aloud *Iggy Peck Architect* by Andrea Beatty. Iggy Peck is a budding architect who loves creating unique structures. His talents are put on hold when a teacher does not share his enthusiasm for building. However, Iggy's teacher soon learns that his skills should be cultivated.

❏ Distribute the Read Aloud Reflection (Handout 4.3). Students should answer the questions on the top half of the page. Then discuss as a class, allowing students an opportunity to add additional information to their answers. Key understandings are outlined in Box 4.1.

❏ Next, explain that the bottom of a 3D structure is called the base. All prisms are named by their base shape. With these instructions, allow students time to complete the bottom half of Handout 4.3. See Figure 4.1 for solutions to these translations.

Teacher's note: The triangular prism's base is a triangle (not a rectangle), which makes the triangular prism fit in the triangle column.

DIMENSIONS

The measurement of length in one direction. Examples: width, depth, and height are dimensions.

ZERO DIMENSIONAL (0-D)	•	A point in space. It has no dimension.
ONE DIMENSIONAL (1-D)	←•••→	A straight line is a set of points which extends. Measured 1 dimension, length.
TWO DIMENSIONAL (2-D)	▪	A flat shape. Measured in 2 dimensions, length and width.
THREE DIMENSIONAL (3-D)	▱	Takes up space. Measured in three dimensions length, width, and height.

Handout 4.3: Read Aloud Reflection

Iggy Peck, Architect by Andrea Beatty

Name: _____

Summarize the main idea of the story.	How does Iggy use dimension?

The base of a 3-D shape is the surface a solid object sits on. Cut out the 3-D shapes. Sort the 3-D shapes under the correct base.

Box 4.1: *Iggy Peck, Architect*
Key Understandings

❏ *Story summary*: Iggy Peck is a budding architect who loves to build and create. His teacher does not think this is a good hobby for a second grader and discourages his love for architecture, until Iggy uses architecture and saves the day!

❏ *Connection to dimension*: Iggy uses dimension when he builds his structures in 3D. For example, he built the bridge, which takes up shape and can be measured in length, width, and height.

Skill Development Activity

❏ Show students the Polyhedrons Anchor Chart (Handout 4.4). Discuss each term on the chart. Display the chart, as students will need to use this terminology during the upcoming lessons.

Teacher's note: Print Handouts 4.5.a–b on cardstock and cut apart the Structure 1–4 cards. You will need enough for students to each have a card.

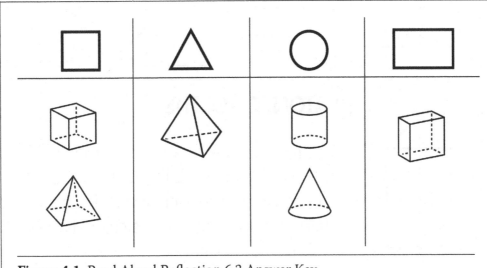

Figure 4.1 Read Aloud Reflection 6.3 Answer Key

POLYHEDRONS

a three-dimensional figure that is formed by polygons
(shapes) that enclose a region in space

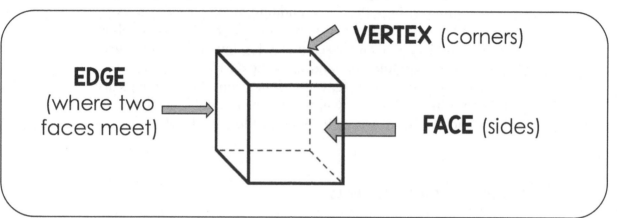

VERTEX (corners)

EDGE
(where two
faces meet)

FACE (sides)

PRISM

A solid shape in which the
top and bottom faces are
the same and all the side
faces are rectangles.

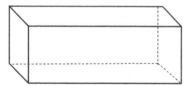

PYRAMID

A solid shape named
after its base which all rise
to a top single point
(apex).

PLATONIC SOLIDS

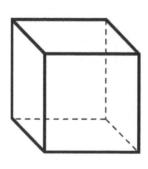

- All faces are the same shape
- Each vertex has the same number
  of edges leading away from it
- The length of every side is the
  same

Structure I

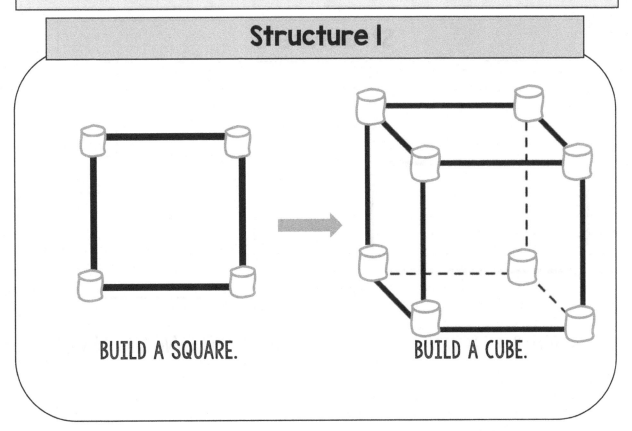

BUILD A SQUARE.

BUILD A CUBE.

Structure 2

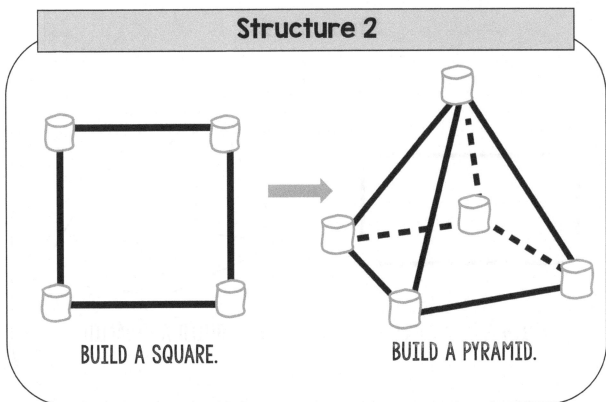

BUILD A SQUARE.

BUILD A PYRAMID.

Handout 4.5b: 2D to 3D

Structure 3

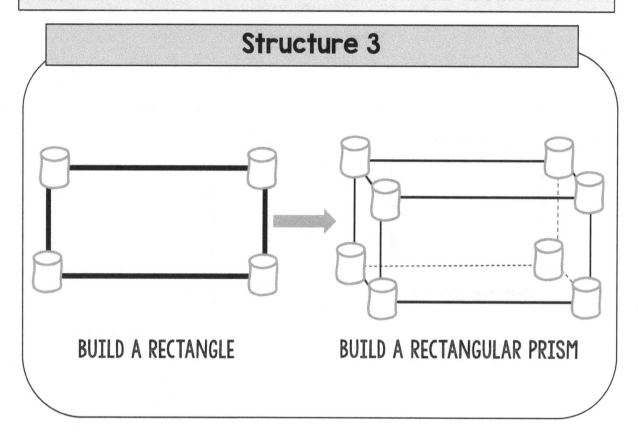

BUILD A RECTANGLE   BUILD A RECTANGULAR PRISM

Structure 4

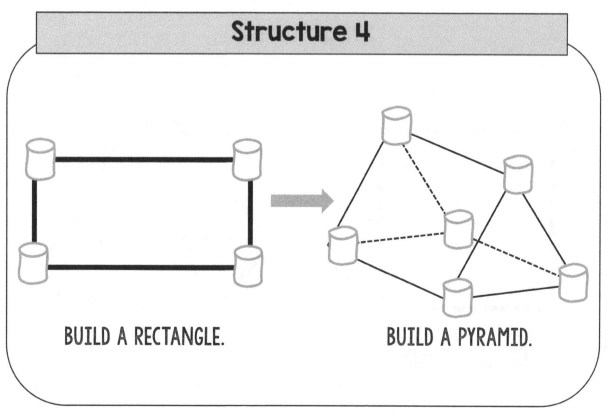

BUILD A RECTANGLE.   BUILD A PYRAMID.

Handout 4.5c: Building Abstract Polyhedrons

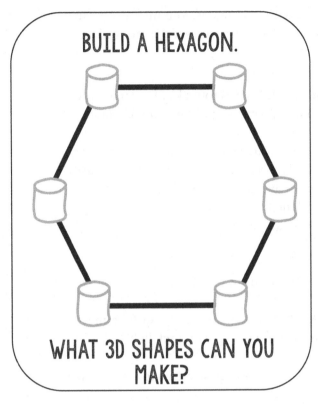

BUILD A HEXAGON.

WHAT 3D SHAPES CAN YOU MAKE?

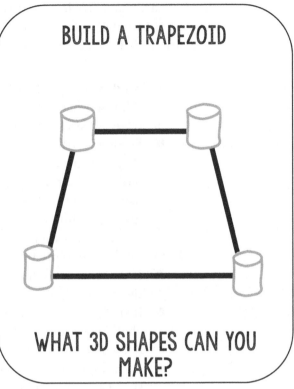

BUILD A TRAPEZOID

WHAT 3D SHAPES CAN YOU MAKE?

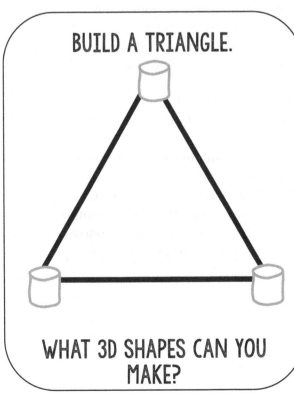

BUILD A TRIANGLE.

WHAT 3D SHAPES CAN YOU MAKE?

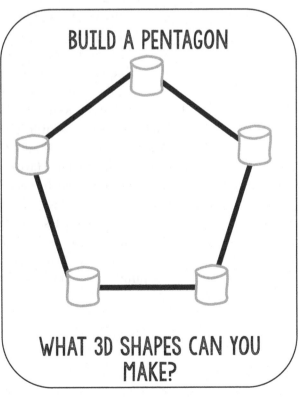

BUILD A PENTAGON

WHAT 3D SHAPES CAN YOU MAKE?

Then students may trade structure cards with classmates. You may also want to copy Handout 4.5.c on cardstock and cut apart the shapes to give to students who are ready for an extension.

❑ Tell students they will be following blueprints to make 3D shapes. You may choose what materials to use, e.g., marshmallows and toothpicks or coffee stir sticks and clay.

■ Students will practice making square and rectangle-based 3D shapes using the Structure 1–4 cards. Circulate while students are building their 3D shapes and have students explain their shapes using the terms from the Polyhedron Anchor Chart. As students finish building their structure, allow students to trade cards and build a new structure.

❑ Option for differentiation:

■ If students are struggling with building the 3D structures, allow them to work in pairs.

■ If students can build the structures with ease and require a more challenging task, distribute the Building Abstract Polyhedrons (Handout 4.5.c).

■ For your most advanced builders: Challenge students to create new structures on their own:

○ Prisms: triangular, hexagonal, pentagonal, or trapezoidal

○ Pyramids: hexagonal, pentagonal, or trapezoidal

○ Platonic solids: tetrahedron (triangular), octahedron (two square pyramids one on top of the other) dodecahedron, (12 sides which are all pentagons)

❑ *Teacher's note*: Keep at least one example of each of the structures that students have built. Use these to introduce the Geometry Prefixes Anchor Chart (Handout 4.6).

❑ Optional Extension: Have students create a building or structure which combines multiple 3D shapes they have created.

❑ To conclude the lesson, share the Geometry Prefixes Anchor Chart with the students. Use the 3D structures to discuss the prefixes using a meaningful context. Students do not need to memorize these prefixes; they just need to be familiar with the concept of the prefixes depicting the number of sides of a shape or 3D structure.

Geometry Prefixes

Prefix	Number of sides
TETRA-	4
PENTA-	5
HEXA	6
HEPTA-	7
OCTA-	8
DECA-	10
DODECA-	12
ICOSA-	20

Exploring Dimensions Lesson 2: Comparing Dimensions

Objective: Explore 1D, 2D, and 3D objects.

Teacher's note: There are many steps to this lesson. Please break this lesson down into manageable sessions for your student population.

Materials

- ❏ Handout 4.6: Geometry Prefixes Anchor Chart (one enlarged from previous lesson)
- ❏ Handout 4.7: Drawing Dimensions (one per student)
- ❏ *Mummy Math* by Cindy Neuschwander (teacher's copy)
- ❏ Handout 4.8: Read Aloud Reflection (one per student)
- ❏ Handout 4.9: Name That Polyhedron (one per student)
- ❏ Figure 4.1: Cube Net
- ❏ Handout 4.10: Foldable Cube Net (one for modeling)
- ❏ Handout 4.11: To Net, or Not to Net (one per student)
- ❏ Handout 4.12: Net Predictions
- ❏ Handouts 4.13.a–j: (Make enough copies for each child to make one 3D figure. Make sure there is at least one example of each figure.)
- ❏ Handout 4.14.a–b: Memory Match Game (one set of cards per two students)

Whole Group Introduction

- ❏ Revisit the Polyhedron Anchor Chart used when creating the 3D shapes in the previous lesson.
- ❏ Explain that these 3D shapes can also be drawn on paper.
- ❏ Distribute the Drawing Dimensions sheet (Handout 4.7). Using a document camera to project and then trace on the board, teach students to draw 3D prisms using the model *shape, duplicate, connect*. Alternately, reproduce the shapes on the handout by drawing them onto the board. In this method, you draw the shape, duplicate the shape a little to the upper right, then connect the vertices with straight lines.

Read Aloud Activity

- ❏ Display the Geometry Prefixes Anchor Chart (Handout 4.6). Remind students that in geometry, there are prefixes used to designate the

Handout 4.7: Drawing Dimensions

Name: _____

SHAPE #1	DUPLICATE	CONNECT

number of sides. This reference anchor chart will be used throughout the lessons.

❏ Introduce the book *Mummy Math* by Cindy Neuschwander. Tell students that this book will reference many of the 3D figures they made in the last lesson. Tell students to be on the lookout for 3D figures and geometry prefixes throughout the book.

❏ Read aloud *Mummy Math* by Cindy Neuschwander. In this story, Matt and Bibi go on an Egyptian exploration. They use their knowledge of geometry to figure out the solution to the mystery.

❏ Distribute the Read Aloud Reflection page (Handout 4.8). Allow students to talk in pairs or small groups about the questions. Remind students to use the Polyhedron Anchor Chart to help with the last question. See Box 4.2 for key understandings to target.

Box 4.2: *Mummy Math* Key Understandings

❏ *Story summary*: Two children traveling through ancient Egypt must use their knowledge of two- and three-dimensional shapes to solve a mystery.

❏ *Connection to dimensions*: Matt and Bibi must use their knowledge of properties of geometric solids in order to escape the pharaoh's tomb.

❏ *Prisms*: rectangular prism, triangular prism

❏ *Pyramids*: square pyramid, hexagonal pyramid

❏ *Platonic solids*: octahedron, dodecahedron

prism	pyramid	platonic solid

Figure 4.2 Read Aloud Reflection 6.8 Answer Key

Handout 4.8: Read Aloud Reflection
Mummy Math by Cindy Neuschwander

Name: _____

Summarize the main idea of the story.	How did the book show dimension?

Cut out the 3-D shape and sort them according to type of polyhedron

prism	pyramid	platonic solid

Skill Development Activity

Teacher's note: Before class, make one cube (Handout 4.10) from the nets provided. This should be copied on cardstock and taped together. In addition, have the nets from Exploring Dimension Lesson 2: To Net or Not to Net? cut out and ready to go for this lesson.

❏ Show students the 3D figures referenced in the book (cube, rectangular prism, triangular prism, square based pyramid, tetrahedron, cone, cylinder, and sphere). You may use purchased 3D shapes or construct your own using the templates provided. One by one, discuss the figures using the terminology *face, vertices,* and *edges.* For example, the cube has 6 faces, 8 vertices, and 12 edges.

❏ Revisit the Geometry Prefixes Anchor Chart (Handout 4.6) along with the Polyhedron Anchor Chart (Handout 4.4) from the previous lessons.

❏ Distribute Name that Polyhedron (Handout 4.9). Explain to the students that the solid shapes are named according to their base shape. Tell students to use the geometry prefixes along with their knowledge of polyhedrons to try and name each polyhedron. Tell students not to glue the shapes down yet.

❏ Review the 3D shape names with students and have them glue down the shapes.

❏ Next, show the students the cardstock cube you pre-made from Handout 4.10. Explain that in the previous lesson, they made 3D solid figures using 2D shapes and plans.

❏ Ask students if they can think of a way to take this 3D solid figure back into a 2D shape?

❏ Put the 3D foldable cardstock cube (Handout 4.10) that you made on top of the cube net (Figure 4.1) and explain that a net is a 2D representation of a 3D figure. Carefully break the cube down to show them how it becomes a 2D net when opened.

❏ Distribute To Net or Not to Net? (Handout 4.11). Have students try to visually manipulate the nets to decide if it is possible to fold each net into a cube. Have students attempt to do this mentally. Ask the students to defend their reasoning and prove that each of the nets can be folded into a cube. After, you can either model the folding of the nets or allow students to cut and fold the nets to determine the correct nets. (Numbers 1, 3, 4, 6, and 8 will form a cube.)

❏ Next, distribute Handout 3.12 to students and discuss the various 2D nets. Ask the students to predict what 3D solid each net will fold into.

Handout 4.9: Name That Polyhedron

Name: _____

Use the Polyhedron Poster and the Prefix Poster, cut and sort the shapes accordingly.

			pentagonal prism	tetrahedron	triangular prism
			pentagonal pyramid	icosahedron	rectangular prism
			octahedron	Hexagonal pyramid	pyramid
			Hexagonal prism	cube	dodecahedron
			cone	cylinder	rhombic prism

Handout 4.10: Foldable Cube Net

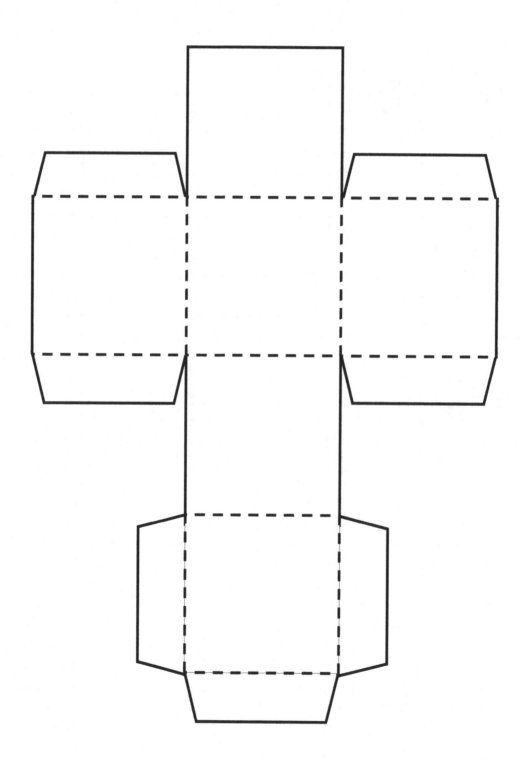

Handout 4.11: To Net, or Not to Net?

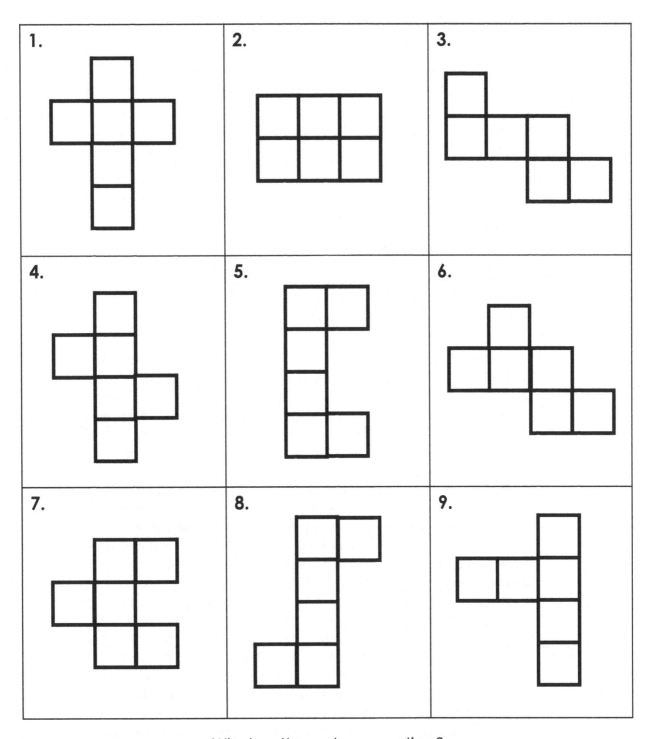

What patterns do you notice?
How can you determine if the net will make a shape?

triangular prism	rectangular prism	pyramid	dodecahedron	rhombic prism
tetrahedron	icosahedron	Hexagonal pyramid	cube	cylinder
pentagonal prism	pentagonal pyramid	octahedron	Hexagonal prism	cone

Figure 4.3 Name that Polyhedron Answer Key

For a challenge, have students label the face of the net that will be the base of the figure. See Figure 4.3 for solutions.

❏ At this point in the lesson, split the class into groups of five to construct the nets provided. We suggest grouping the students heterogeneously and dividing the shapes by difficulty of folding, so that students with less developed fine motor skills are given the less complex nets to fold.
  ■ Cube, cone, cylinder (easy)
  ■ Tetrahedron, triangular prism, rectangular prism (easy/medium)
  ■ Rhombic prism, pentagonal prism, hexagonal prism (medium)
  ■ Pentagonal pyramid, hexagonal pyramid, pyramid (medium/hard)
  ■ Dodecahedron, octahedron, icosahedron (hard)
❏ Have groups make at least one of each shape (they can make more if time permits). Then each group will create a structure using all the 3D shapes at least once.
❏ *Teacher's note*: Set aside a completed example of each of the 3D figures made in this lesson for reference in Sub-Skill 5: Seeking Structure.
❏ Optional Activity: Students will cut out the Memory Match Game cards (Handout 4.14.a–b). They should flip them over and place in an array. Taking turns, students will select two cards and determine if the net will form the shape. If they match, students will keep the two cards. Continue until all matches have been made. The student with the most matches wins.

Handout 4.12: Net Predictions

Look at each net, predict the 3-D solid it will become & record your predictions in the box.
CHALLENGE: Write a B on the face you think will be the base when this shape is made.

Rhombic prism	Rectangular prism	Octahedron
Dodecahedron	Tetrahedron	Hexagonal pyramid
Pentagonal prism	Triangular prism	Icosahedron
Pentagonal pyramid	pyramid	Hexagonal prism

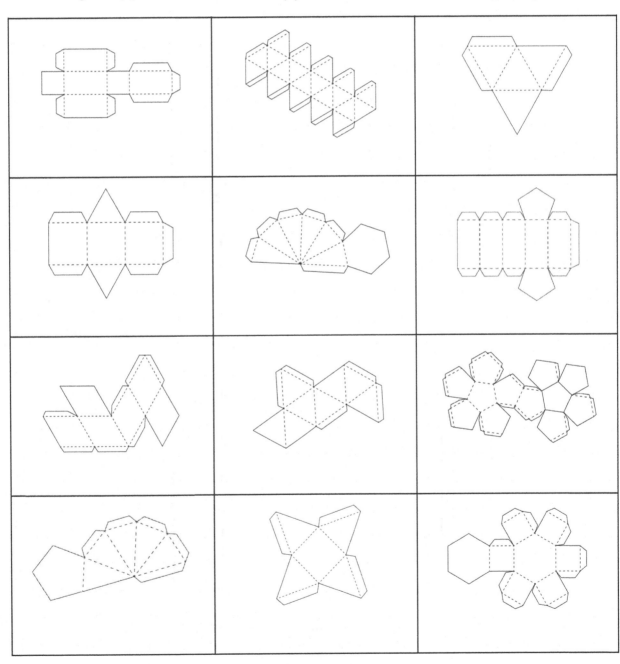

Handout 4.13.a: Triangular Prism Net

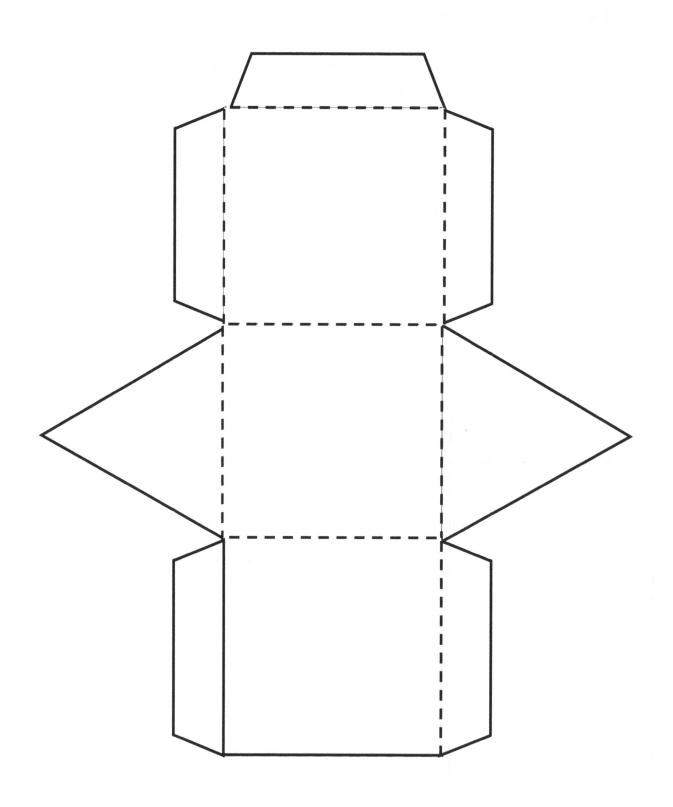

Handout 4.13.b: Tetrahedron Net

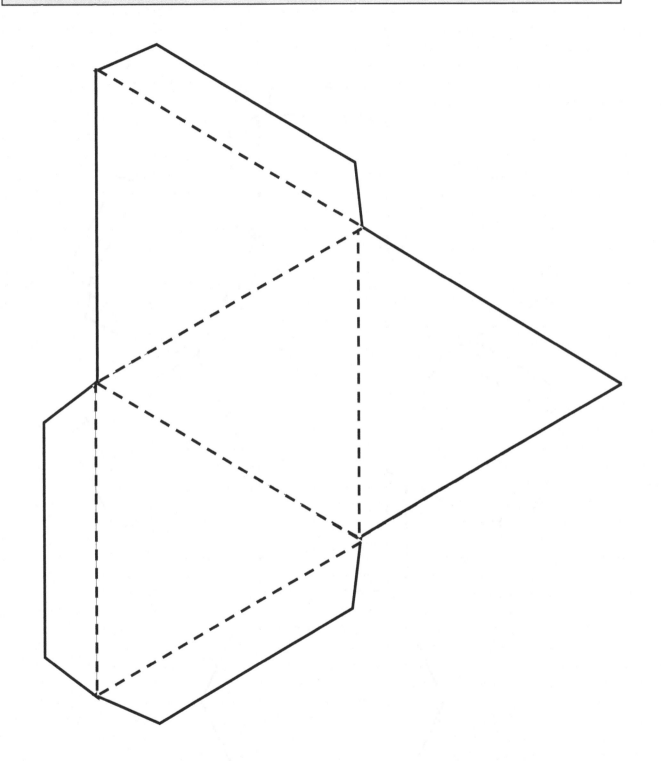

Handout 4.13.c: Hexagonal Prism Net

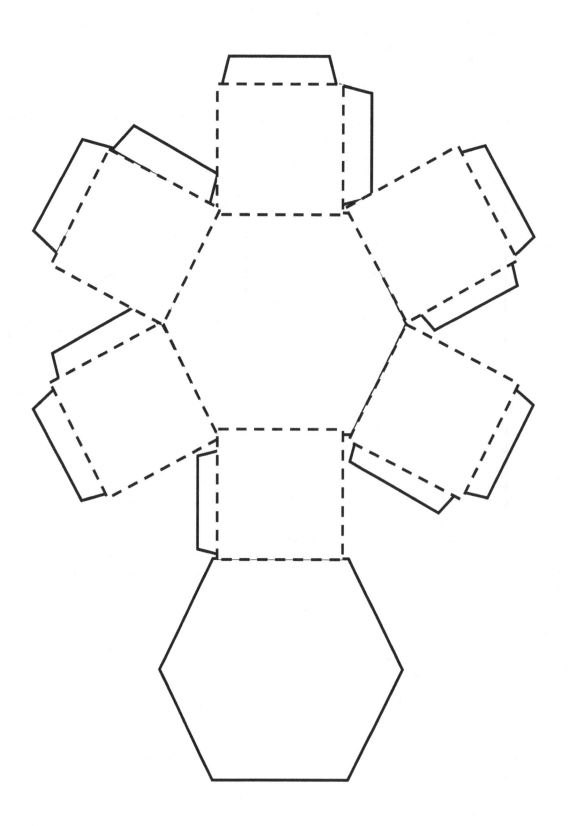

Handout 4.13.d: Hexagonal Pyramid Net

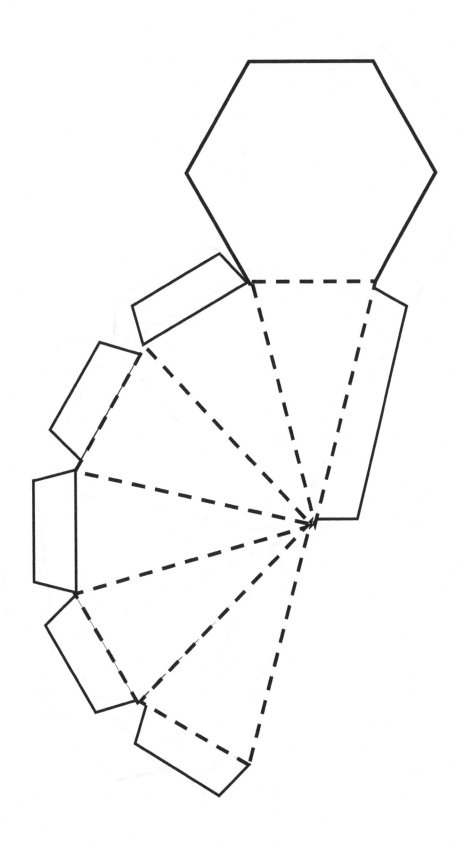

Handout 4.13.e: Pentagonal Pyramid Net

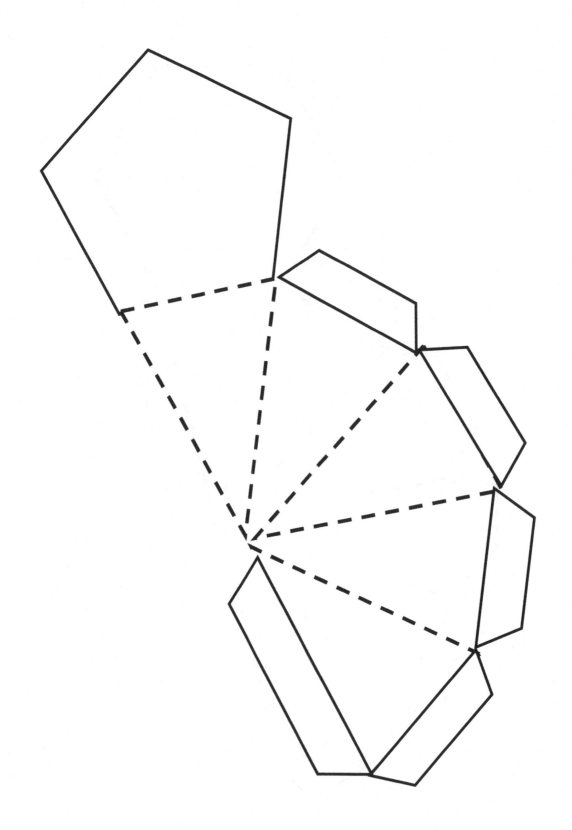

Handout 4.13.f: Pentagonal Prism Net

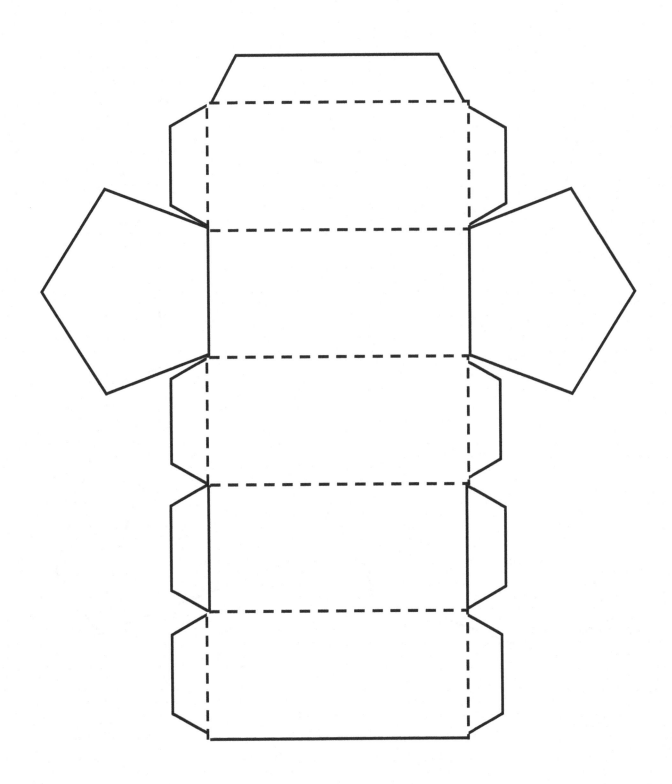

Handout 4.13.g: Square Pyramid Net

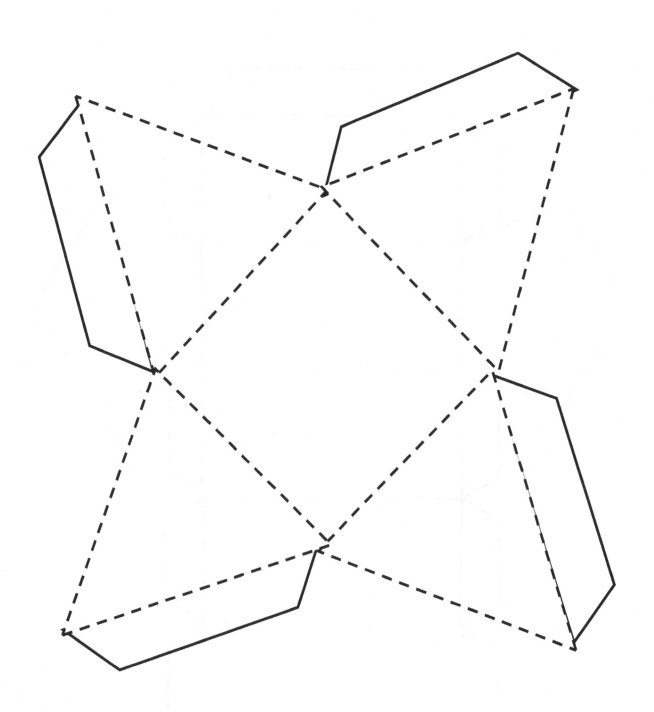

Handout 4.13.h: Rectangular Prism Net

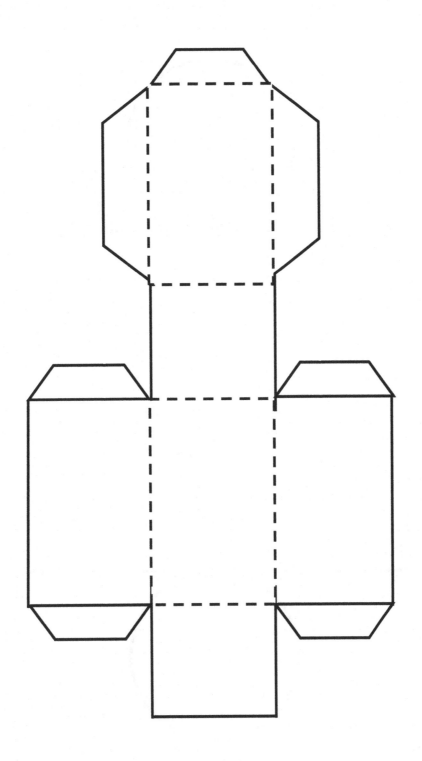

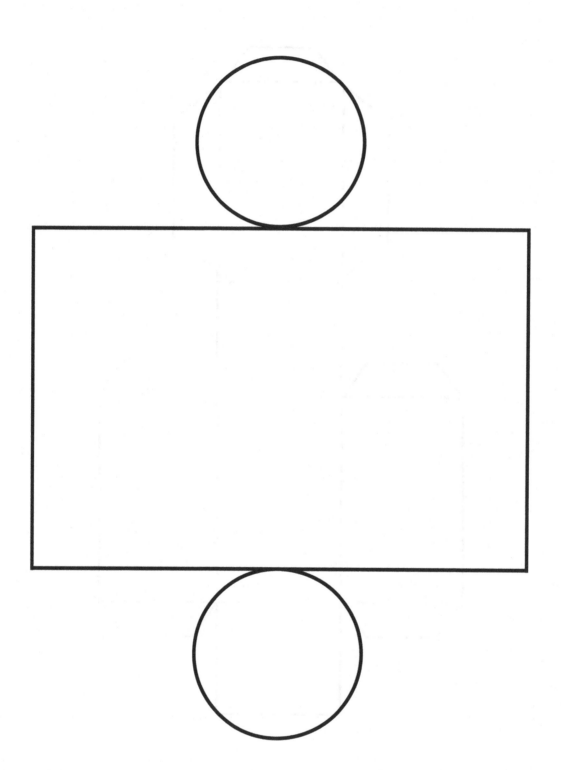

Handout 4.13.j: Cone Net

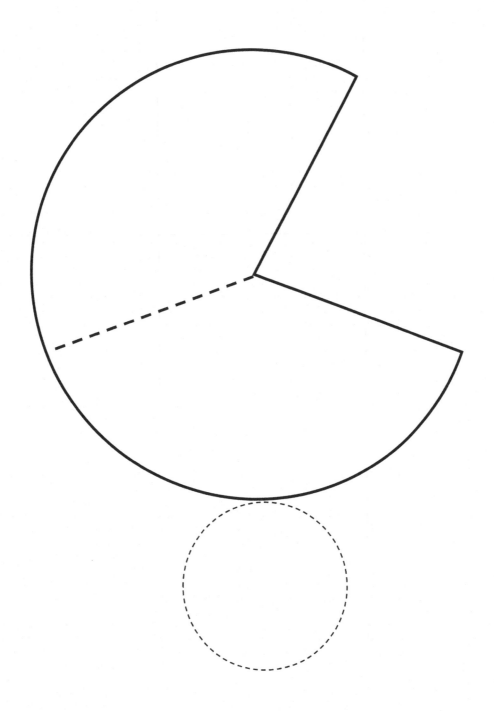

Handout 4.14.a: Net Memory Match

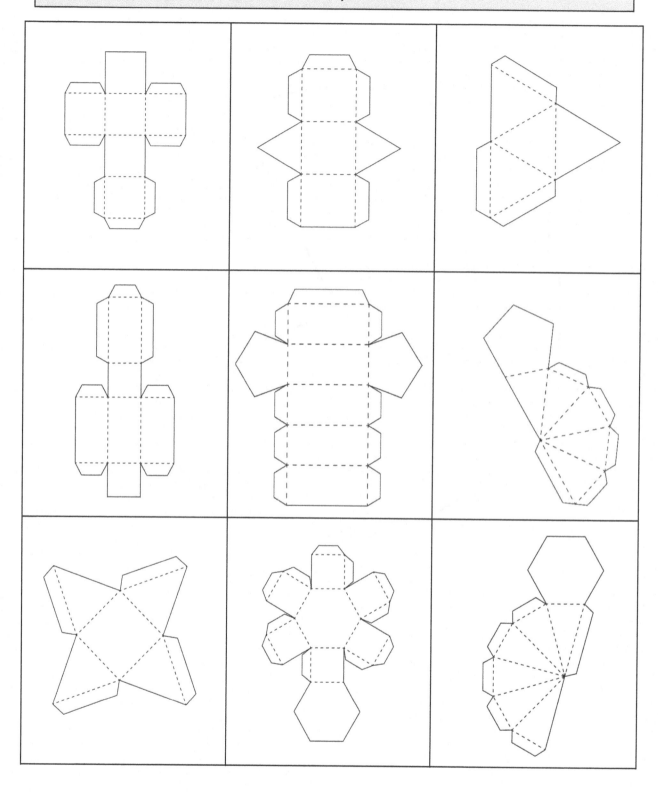

Handout 4.14.b: Net Memory Match

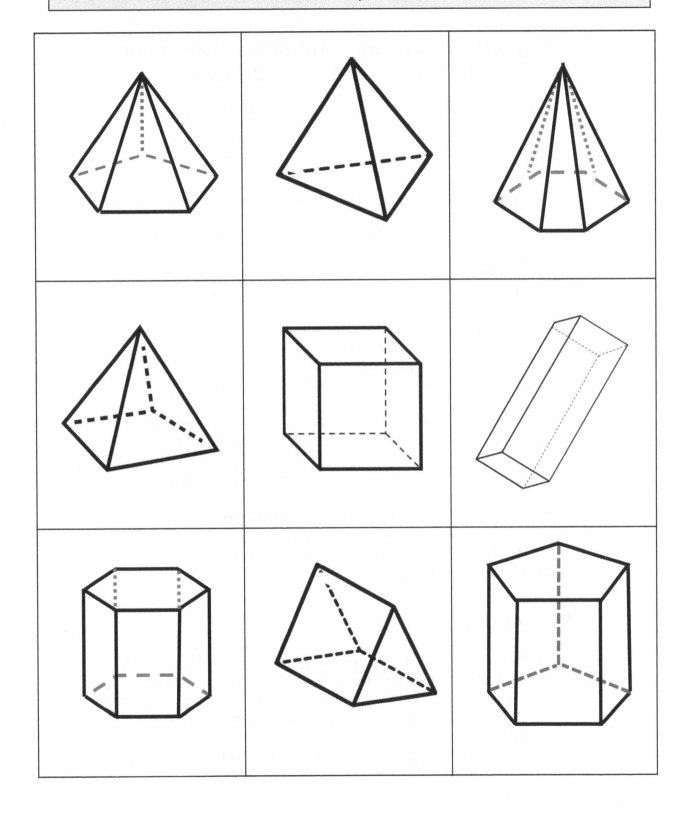

Exploring Dimensions Authentic Application Activity: The Math of Origami

Objective: Investigate the spatial and mathematical laws of origami.

Materials

- ❏ Handout 4.15: Origami Symbols Anchor Chart (one enlarged copy for the class)
- ❏ Handout 4.16: Origami Rules Anchor Chart (one enlarged copy for the class)
- ❏ Handout 4.17: Directed Folding Template—House (one per student)
- ❏ Handout 4.18: Directed Folding Instructions—House (one enlarged copy for the class)
- ❏ Optional: *Origami House Folding* video:
  - ■ https://www.youtube.com/watch?v=MjpV9Sy1KK8
- ❏ *The Unexpected Math of Origami* video
  - ■ https://ed.ted.com/lessons/the-unexpected-math-of-origami-evan-zodl
- ❏ Handout 4.19: Origami Rules Proof—House (one per student)
- ❏ Handout 4.20: Origami Application Template—Windmill (one per student)
- ❏ Handout 4.21: Origami Application Instructions—Windmill (one per student)
- ❏ Handout 4.22: Origami Application Proof (one per student)
- ❏ Optional: *Origami Windmill Folding* video link:
  - ■ https://www.youtube.com/watch?v=0sJVhKBoqFc
- ❏ Scissors for each student

Read Aloud Activity

- ❏ Review the exploring dimension anchor chart (Handout 4.1), reminding students that this includes visualizing and constructing objects. Tell students that in this book, the main character uses visualizing and tries to construct objects, although it's not as easy as it seems.
- ❏ Read aloud *More-igami* by Dori Kleber. Pause to discuss how origami takes a 2D piece of paper and, through folding patterns, turns it into a 3D object.

Skill Development: Authentic Application

Teacher's note: Before completing this next section, it is highly encouraged that you practice folding each of the origami shapes. It is also helpful to watch the videos prior to teaching this lesson, as the material can be difficult at first.

- ❏ Explain that origami is both art and math, as it's a pattern of creases.
- ❏ Show students the Origami Symbols Anchor Chart (Handout 4.15). Explain each action on the anchor chart by modeling the folding.
- ❏ Cut out the square house pattern. Without telling the students what it will become, show the students the crease patterns for the house, using the Directed Folding Template—House (Handout 4.17). Ask students to predict what this may be?
- ❏ Distribute the Directed Folding Template—House (Handout 4.17) to each student. Tell students to carefully cut out the square. Tell students they will be folding this square into a house. Instruct students to fold the paper with the lines side down. They will use the lines as guides when folding. Next provide the directions to make the house either using the Directed Folding Instructions—House (Handout 4.18) or using the YouTube easy origami house video as a guide.
  - ■ https://www.youtube.com/watch?v=MjpV9Sy1KK8
- ❏ As students are folding their houses, walk around aiding those who are struggling. When adept students finish their houses, allow them to help other students. Each student will need their own house to complete the remainder of the lesson.
- ❏ Share the following video on the unexpected math of origami by Evan Zodl. Link: https://ed.ted.com/lessons/the-unexpected-math-of-origami-evan-zodl Tell students to pay close attention to the Four Rules for origami folding.
- ❏ Display the Origami Rules Anchor Chart (Handout 4.16) as you guide students through investigating the Four Rules. Using your origami house, show students the following rules while modeling how to complete the Origami Rules Proof—House page (Handout 4.19) after each rule.

Teacher's note: We recommend modeling the Four Rules using your origami house. Students may keep theirs folded and will record their answers on the Origami Rules Proof page (Handout 4.19).

- ❏ **Law 1—Maekawa's Theorem:** At any vertex, the number of valley and mountain folds always differ by two, meaning that the number of mountain folds (the fold points upward) and valley (fold points down)

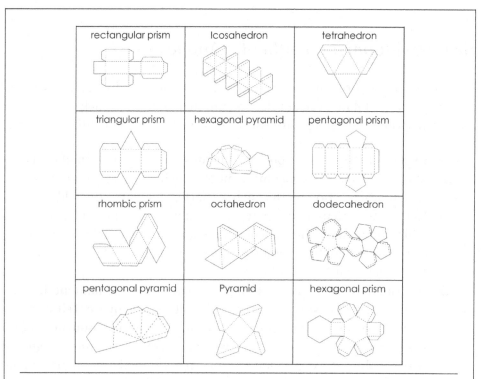

Figure 4.4 Net Prediction Answer Key

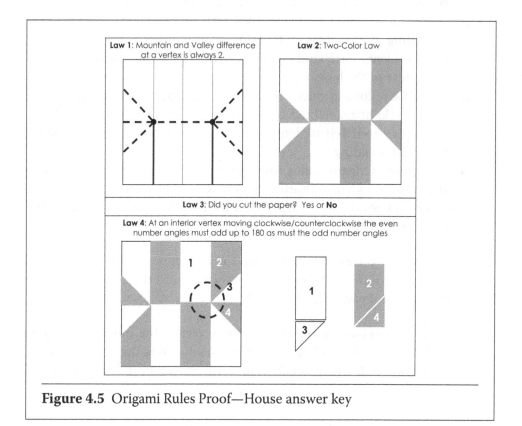

Figure 4.5 Origami Rules Proof—House answer key

Origami Symbols

CREASES

The **dotted lines** show where to fold.

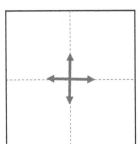

The **solid lines** show the crease after the folds.

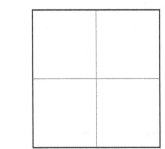

FOLDS

Mountain folds are convex, they stick up like mountains.

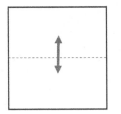

Valley folds are concave, they go down like a valley.

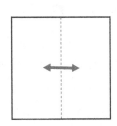 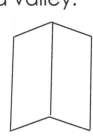

ARROWS

The **arrows** indicate the direction to fold.

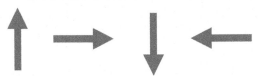

The **double arrows** indicate a crease that is to be folded and then unfolded.

Origami RULES

MAEKAWA'S THEOREM

at any vertex, the number of valley and mountain folds always differ by two.

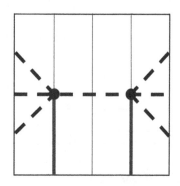

TWO-COLOR RULE

the regions between the creases can be colored with two colors

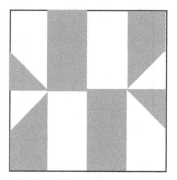

A SHEET CAN NEVER PENETRATE A FOLD

no matter how many times you try to stack folds and sheets, a sheet can never penetrate a fold AND NO CUTTING.

KAWASAKI'S THEOREM

at any vertex, the sum of all the odd angles adds up to 180 degrees, as do the even.

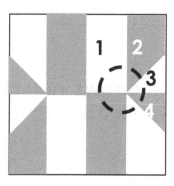

Handout 4.17: Directed Folding Template-House

Carefully cut out the square below. Follow the teacher's directions to fold this 2-dimensional flat foldable base into a final 3-dimensional shape.

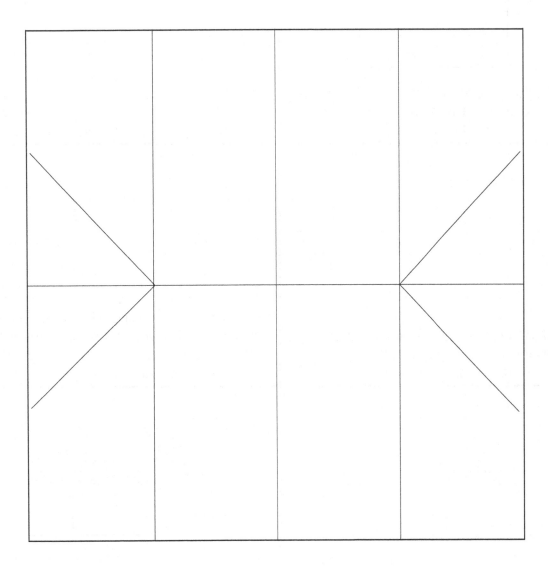

Handout 4.18: Directed Folding Instructions-House

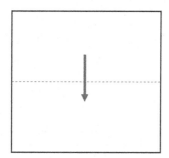

Fold the paper in half by bringing the top edge to the bottom edge and make a crease.

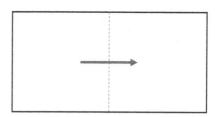

Fold in half from left to right and make a light crease. Then open the fold.

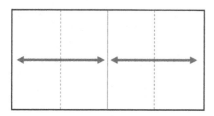

Fold the right edge to meet the center fold and make a crease. Then do the same thing to the right.

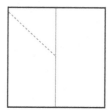

Notice the two flaps with meet in the middle. Slide your finger into the left opening and carefully pull to the left, it becomes a triangle.

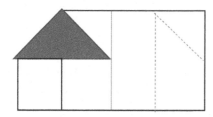

Line up the crease of the triangle to the crease in the square going down. Then crease the triangle to make the left side roof.

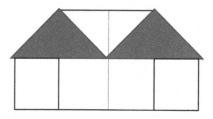

Do the same thing to the right side to make the house.

Handout 4.19: Origami Rules Proof-House

Name: _____

Law 1: Mountain and Valley difference at a vertex is always 2.

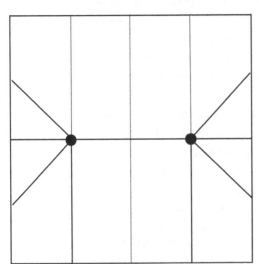

Law 2: Two-Color Law

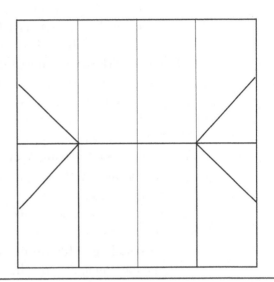

Law 3: Did you cut the paper?   Yes or No

Law 4: At an interior vertex moving clockwise/counterclockwise the even number angles must add up to 180 as must the odd number angles

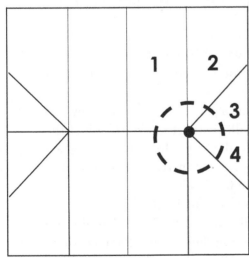

subtracted will always equal two. For example, on the house, there are three mountains and one valley at each vertex; 3 − 1 = 2.

- Have students take out two different colored markers. Guide students through tracing the outside mountains of the house in one color (blue). Then have them open the two inside flaps of the house and color the valleys a different color (red).

❏ **Law 2—The Two-Color Rule:** The regions between the creases can be colored with two colors. Using your origami house, show students how to alternate using two colors to complete the two-color law. On the worksheet, students will color the crease pattern with just two alternating colors without ever having the same color meet.

❏ **Law 3—No Cutting:** A sheet may never penetrate a fold, which means you cannot cut the paper to make the folds work. Discuss with students how in origami the paper is not cut to fit; the folds create the structures.

❏ **Law 4—Kawasaki's Theorem:** If you number all angles at an interior vertex moving clockwise/counterclockwise, the even number angles must add up to 180°, as must the odd number angles. Model numbering and cutting apart your house. Using four angles, prove that the evens and odds add up to 180°. Students will cut out the four shapes at the bottom of the page to prove Kawasaki's theorem.

Teacher's note: This may be where you choose to stop the lesson for your student population. However, if your students are ready for a challenge, continue with the following origami application lesson.

❏ Distribute Origami Application Template—Windmill (Handout 4.20). Tell students they will follow the same procedure using a different origami pattern.

❏ Direct students to carefully cut out the square. Tell students they will be folding this square into a windmill. Instruct students to fold the paper with the lines side down. They will use the lines as guides when folding. Next provide the Origami Application Instructions—Windmill (Handout 4.21) or use the origami windmill video as a guide.
- https://www.youtube.com/watch?v=0sJVhKBoqFc

❏ As students are folding their windmills, walk around aiding those who are struggling. When adept students finish their windmills, allow them to help other students. Each student will need their own windmill to complete the remainder of the lesson.

❏ Model tracing the mountain and valley folds using the final product. Then unfold the paper to use on the worksheet.

❏ Distribute the Origami Application Proof—Windmill page (Handout 4.22).

Handout 4.20: Origami Application Template: Windmill

Carefully cut out the square below. Follow the teacher's directions to fold this 2-dimensional flat foldable base into a final 3-dimensional shape.

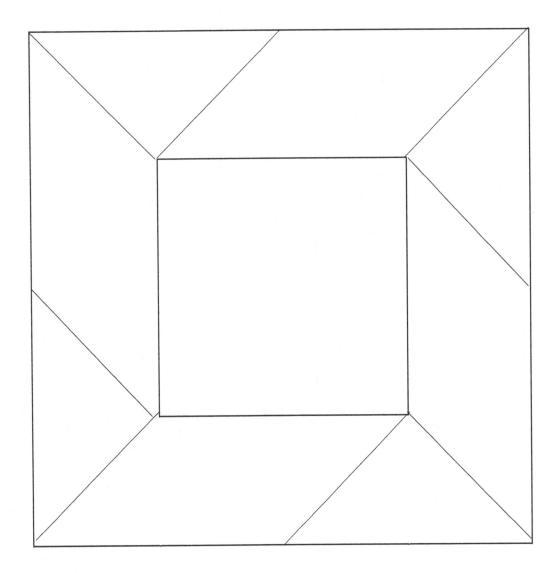

Handout 4.21: Origami Application Instructions: Windmill

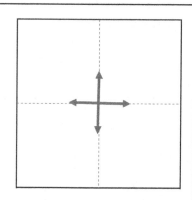

Fold the paper in half both directions and unfold.

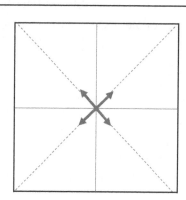

Fold the paper diagonally both directions and unfold.

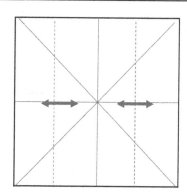

Fold both sides into the center to meet the center line.

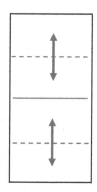

Fold the top and bottom edges to meet the middle crease.

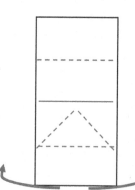

Open the paper the fold along the dotted lines.

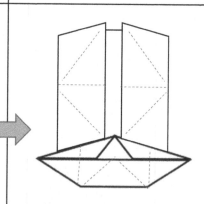

Squash the fold flat. Do the same to the opposite side.

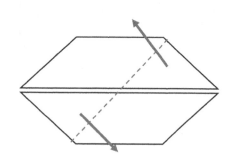

Fold the paper out along the dotted lines.

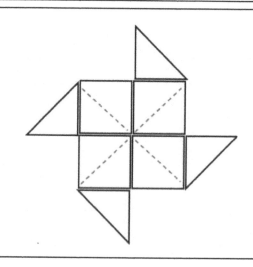

Handout 4.22: Origami Application Proof- Windmill

Name: _____

Law 1: Mountain and Valley difference at a vertex is always 2.

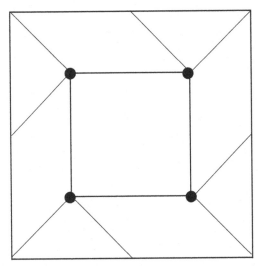

Law 2: Two-Color Law

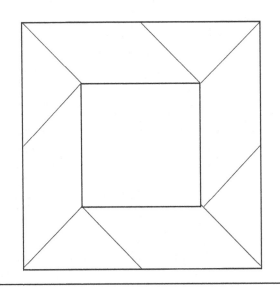

Law 3: Did you cut the paper? Yes or No

Law 4: At an interior vertex moving clockwise/counterclockwise the even number angles must add up to 180 as must the odd number angles

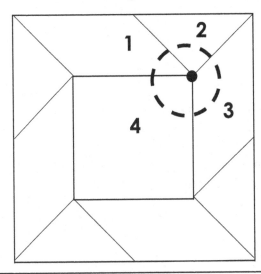

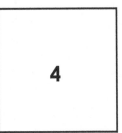

4

1

2

3

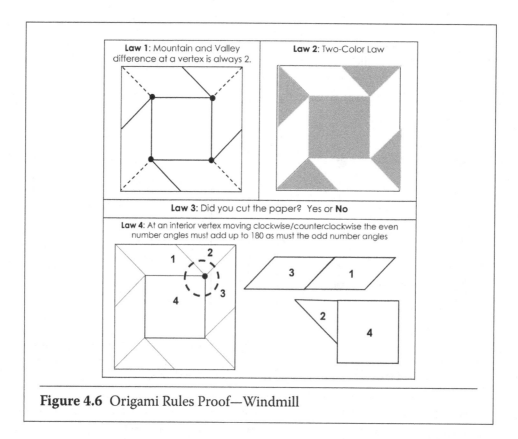

Figure 4.6 Origami Rules Proof—Windmill

- ❏ Allow students the opportunity to complete the Origami Rule Proof—Windmill page on their own. If they are struggling, students may work with a partner or in a small group.
- ❏ Discuss the concepts of dimension.
  - ■ Describe 0D, 1D, 2D, and 3D.
  - ■ How does visualizing help you construct objects?
  - ■ How is it possible to turn something 2D into something 3D?
  - ■ Is it possible to turn something from 1D to 3D? How?
- ❏ Optional Extension: Have students make the origami ladybug using the provided instructions from the book *More-igami*. Then, students can try and prove the Four Rules on their origami ladybug.
- ❏ Have students copy the fold patterns on their worksheet noting the mountain vs. valley folds.

Exploring Dimensions Concluding Activities

- ❏ Conclude the chapter on Exploring Dimensions with the Exploring Dimensions Exit Ticket (Appendix A). Ask students to reflect on their learning about the skill of visualizing and constructing objects. Allow time for students to complete the exit ticket. Use this as a formative assessment to gain a better understanding of your students' readiness to effectively practice the skill of exploring dimension.

❏ If desired, complete the Group Exploring Dimensions Rubric (Appendix A) to track students' progress with the skill.

❏ If desired, use the Visual-Spatial Thinking Student Observation Rubric (Appendix A) to assess and quantify individual students' mastery.

❏ Ask students to retrieve their Visual-Spatial Thinking Avatar (Handout I.3). In the Exploring Dimensions box, they should either write the main ideas of this section or illustrate their avatar using the skill of visualizing and constructing objects.

Bibliography

Beaty, A., and Roberts, D. (2007). *Iggy Peck, architect*. New York: Abrams Books for Young Readers.

Kleber, D. (2016). *More-igami*. Somerville, MA: Candlewick Press.

Neuschwander, C. (2005). *Mummy math: An adventure in geometry*. New York: Henry Holt and Company.

Origami.me. (July 12, 2018). The mathematics, laws, and theory behind crease patterns. https://origami.me/crease-pattern-theory/.

Origami Twist. (December 25, 2019). Easy origami house [video]. *YouTube*. https://www.youtube.com/watch?v=MjpV9Sy1KK8.

Tavin's Origami Instructions. (July 16, 2017). Windmill base origami instructions [video]. *YouTube*. https://www.youtube.com/watch?v=0sJVhKBoqFc.

Zodl, E. (n.d.). The unexpected math of origami [video]. *TED Ed*. https://ed.ted.com/lessons/the-unexpected-math-of-origami-evan-zodl.

CHAPTER 5

Sub-Skill 5

Seeking Structure

TABLE 5.1

Seeking Structure Sub-Skill Overview

Thinking Skill Outline	
Focus Questions	❏ How can we compare objects to identify similarities and differences? ❏ How do disciplinarians use structure?
Lesson 1	*Coordinate Grids* ❏ **Trade Book Focus:** *A Fly on the Ceiling* by Julie Glass ❏ **Practice Activity:** Coordinate Grid Pictures
Lesson 2	*The Four-Color Theorem* ❏ **Trade Book Focus:** *There's a Map on My Lap* by Tish Rabe ❏ **Practice Activity:** Using four colors on a map
Authentic Application Activity	*Euler's Circuits* ❏ **Trade Book Focus:** *Sir Cumference and the Sword in the Cone* by Cindy Neuschwander ❏ **Practice Activity:** Euler's Paths

DOI: 10.4324/9781003267942-6

Seeking Structure Lesson 1:
Coordinate Grids

Objective: Develop strategies for organizing visual information.

Materials

- ❏ Handout 5.1: Seeking Structure Anchor Chart (one enlarged for the class)
- ❏ Handout 5.2: Mystery Vertex Grid (teacher's copy)
- ❏ *A Fly on the Ceiling* by Julie Glass (teacher's copy)
- ❏ Handout 5.3: Read Aloud Reflection (one per student)
- ❏ Handout 5.4.a: Mystery Picture 1 (one per student)
- ❏ Handout 5.4.b: Mystery Picture 2 (duplicate as needed)
- ❏ Handout 5.4.c: Mystery Picture 3 (2 pages) (duplicate as needed)
- ❏ Handout 5.4.d: Mystery Picture 4 (2 pages) (duplicate as needed)

Whole Group Introduction

- ❏ Ask students: What does the word *structure* mean? How can we relate structure to visual thinking?
- ❏ Introduce the Seeking Structure Anchor Chart (Handout 5.1). Explain that when we look for visual patterns and repetitions, our minds are seeking structure.

Read Aloud Activity

- ❏ Fold Handout 5.2 in half. Show students only the top half for now, the Mystery Vertex Grid. (Keep the bottom half of the page covered.) Explain the grid: lines run horizontally and vertically. Tell students that the place where the lines cross is called a vertex. Tell students that you have a secret specific vertex in mind. Invite students to try and explain which vertex they think you have chosen. Students will quickly see that it is difficult to specify the vertex without a way to label points on the grid.
- ❏ Tell them that today you will read a story about a man who discovered a way to label the vertices so that it's easy to determine the specific locations on a grid.

SEEKING STRUCTURE

LOOKING FOR REPETITION AND PATTERNS

Handout 5.2: Mystery Vertex Grid

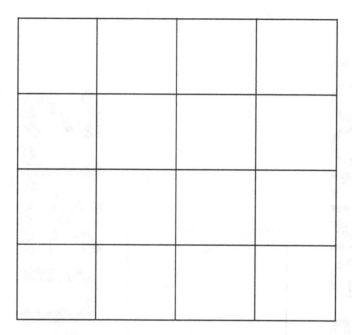

Labeled Mystery Vertex Grid

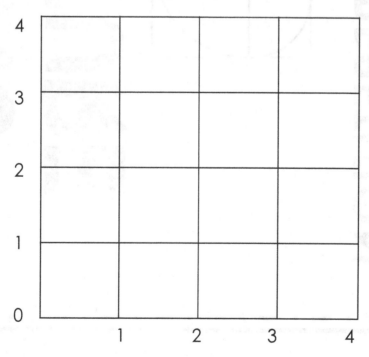

- ❏ Read aloud *A Fly on the Ceiling* by Julie Glass. This funny and accessible story is based on one of math's greatest myths, about Rene Descartes, a French mathematician who popularized the coordinate grid system.
- ❏ After reading the book, show the Labeled Coordinate Grid half page (the bottom half of Handout 5.2). Tell students that you have a secret specific vertex in mind. Invite students to try and explain which vertex they think you have chosen. Remind them to give the directions in (x, y) order. They should be able to locate the vertex utilizing the coordinates. Ask students which grid was easier to use to locate the correct vertex, and why.
- ❏ Distribute the Read Aloud Reflection page (Handout 5.3). Direct students to carefully consider and answer the questions on the top half. Allow students to talk in pairs or small groups. When students have finished, discuss responses as a whole group.
- ❏ Direct students to the bottom half of the page, and model placing dot A on the coordinate grid. Then allow those students who demonstrate strong understanding and are ready to move on the opportunity to complete on their own, while you continue to model the plotting process for the rest. See key understandings for the read aloud in Box 5.1.

Box 5.1: *A Fly on the Ceiling* Key Understandings

- ❏ Rene Descartes was a French mathematician who popularized the Cartesian system of coordinates. This is a fictional tale based on one of math's greatest myths: that Descartes invented the Cartesian system while lying in bed and watching a fly land on the ceiling. He then wanted to figure out a system to see if the fly would land in the same spot twice.
- ❏ The structure of identifying points on a coordinate grid is important in understanding how the Cartesian system works.

Skill Development Activity

- ❏ Distribute Mystery Picture 1 (Handout 5.2.a). Then display the Mystery Picture 1 (Handout 5.2.a) using a document camera. Explain that you will be modeling how to draw a mystery picture by following

Handout 5.3: Read Aloud Reflection

A Fly on the Ceiling by Julie Glass

Name: _____

Summarize the main idea of the story.	How did the book show structure?

Put the following coordinates on the grid below. Place a dot on the vertex and label it with the accompanying letter.

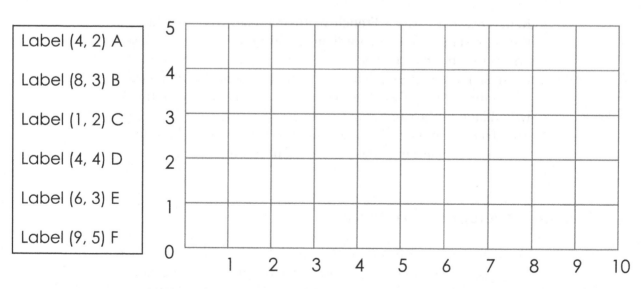

Label (4, 2) A

Label (8, 3) B

Label (1, 2) C

Label (4, 4) D

Label (6, 3) E

Label (9, 5) F

Handout 5.4a: Mystery Picture 1

Name: _____

Plot the points on the coordinate grid.
Then connect the points with lines to complete a hidden picture.

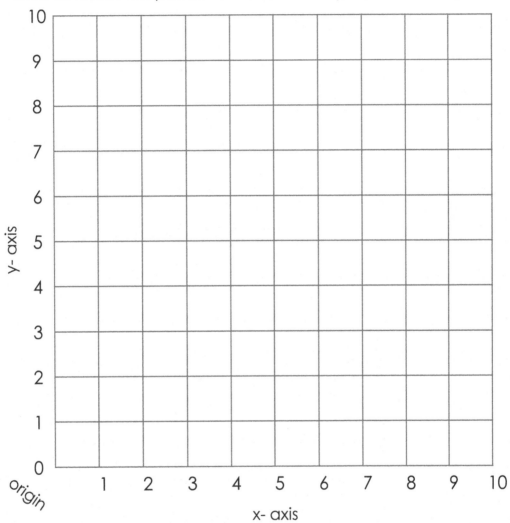

Line 1	**Line 2**	**Line 3**	**Line 4**	**Line 5**
❑(2, 0)	❑(2, 6)	❑ (3, 7)	❑ (3, 4)	❑ (5, 0)
❑(2, 6)	❑(5, 10)	❑ (3, 10)	❑ (3, 5)	❑ (5, 3)
❑(8, 6)	❑(8, 6)	❑ (4, 10)	❑ (7, 5)	❑ (7, 3)
❑(8. 0)		❑ (4, 9)	❑ (7, 4)	❑ (7, 0)
❑(2, 0)			❑(3, 4)	

Handout 5.4b: Mystery Picture 2

Plot the points on the coordinate grid.
Then connect the points with lines to complete a hidden picture.

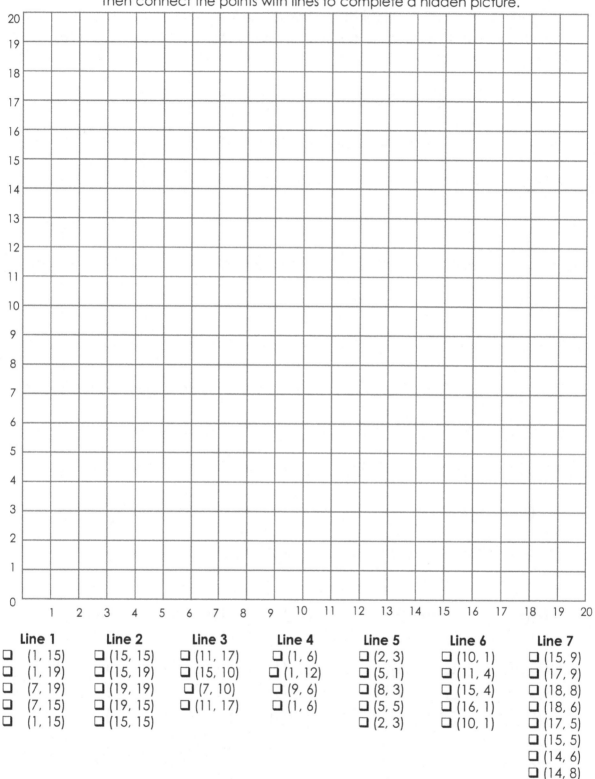

Line 1	Line 2	Line 3	Line 4	Line 5	Line 6	Line 7
❏ (1, 15)	❏ (15, 15)	❏ (11, 17)	❏ (1, 6)	❏ (2, 3)	❏ (10, 1)	❏ (15, 9)
❏ (1, 19)	❏ (15, 19)	❏ (15, 10)	❏ (1, 12)	❏ (5, 1)	❏ (11, 4)	❏ (17, 9)
❏ (7, 19)	❏ (19, 19)	❏ (7, 10)	❏ (9, 6)	❏ (8, 3)	❏ (15, 4)	❏ (18, 8)
❏ (7, 15)	❏ (19, 15)	❏ (11, 17)	❏ (1, 6)	❏ (5, 5)	❏ (16, 1)	❏ (18, 6)
❏ (1, 15)	❏ (15, 15)			❏ (2, 3)	❏ (10, 1)	❏ (17, 5)
						❏ (15, 5)
						❏ (14, 6)
						❏ (14, 8)
						❏ (15, 9)

Handout 5.4c: Mystery Picture 3

Name: _____

Plot the points on the coordinate grid.
Then connect the points with lines to complete a hidden picture.

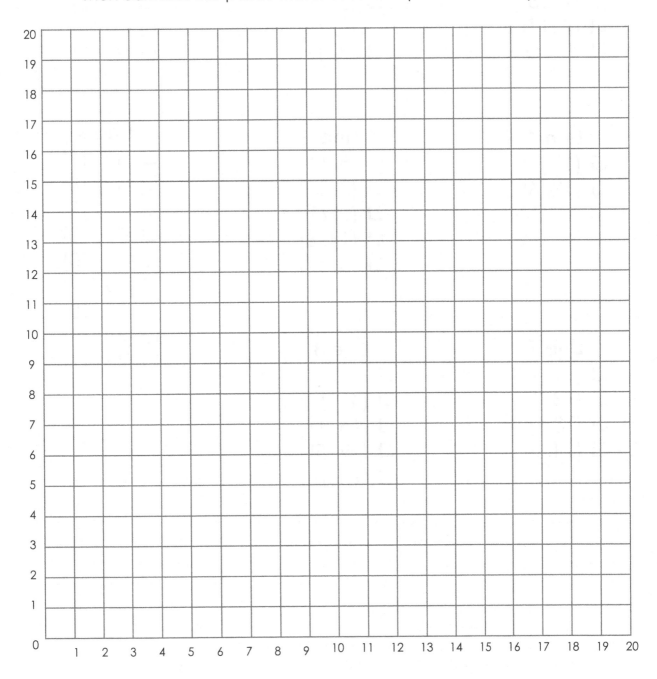

Handout 5.4c: Mystery Picture 3, continued

Line 1
- ❑ (1, 18)
- ❑ (2, 17)
- ❑ (3, 18)

Line 2
- ❑ (2, 16)
- ❑ (3, 15)
- ❑ (4, 16)

Line 3
- ❑ (4, 17)
- ❑ (5, 16)
- ❑ (6, 17)

Line 4
- ❑ (13, 5)
- ❑ (13, 6)

Line 5
- ❑ (8, 5)
- ❑ (8, 19)
- ❑ (2, 6)
- ❑ (14, 6)
- ❑ (8, 19)

Line 6
- ❑ (17, 17)
- ❑ (16, 18)
- ❑ (16, 19)
- ❑ (17, 20)
- ❑ (18, 20)
- ❑ (19, 19)
- ❑ (19, 18)
- ❑ (18, 17)
- ❑ (17, 17)

Line 7
- ❑ (11, 13)
- ❑ (13, 17)
- ❑ (18,6)
- ❑ (14, 6)

Line 8
- ❑ (1, 5)
- ❑ (4, 1)
- ❑ (16, 1)
- ❑ (19, 5)
- ❑ (1, 5)

Handout 5.4d: Mystery Picture 4

Name: _____

Plot the points on the coordinate grid.
Then connect the points with lines to complete a hidden picture.

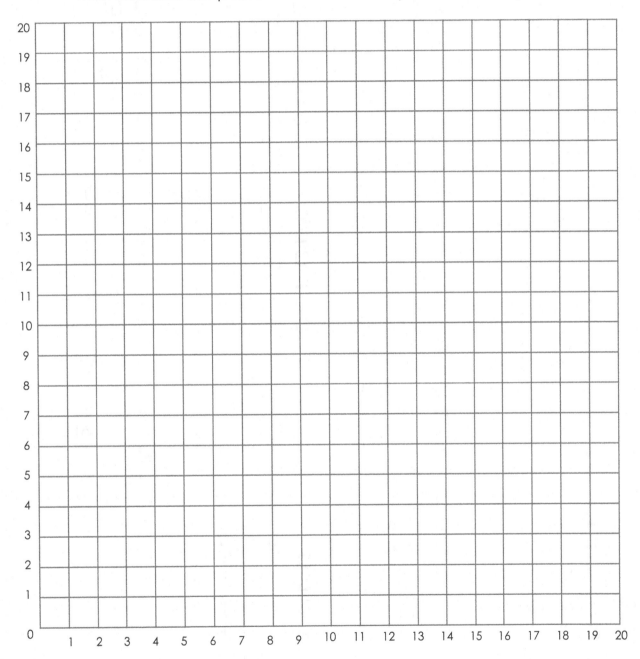

Handout 5.4d: Mystery Picture 4, continued

Line 1
- ❑ (8, 10)
- ❑ (9, 10)
- ❑ (9, 8)
- ❑ (8, 8)
- ❑ (8, 10)

Line 2
- ❑ (3, 13)
- ❑ (5, 10)
- ❑ (2, 10)
- ❑ (2, 9)
- ❑ (3, 9)
- ❑ (3, 8)
- ❑ (2, 8)
- ❑ (2, 10)
- ❑ (1, 10)
- ❑ (3, 13)
- ❑ (3, 15)
- ❑ (1, 14)
- ❑ (3, 14)

Line 3
- ❑ (4, 10)
- ❑ (4, 6)
- ❑ (5, 6)
- ❑ (5, 7)
- ❑ (7, 7)
- ❑ (7, 12)
- ❑ (6, 12)
- ❑ (6, 14)
- ❑ (7, 14)
- ❑ (7, 13)
- ❑ (8, 13)
- ❑ (8, 14)

Line 4
- ❑ (15, 7)
- ❑ (14, 7)
- ❑ (14, 6)
- ❑ (13, 6)
- ❑ (13, 7)
- ❑ (12, 7)
- ❑ (12, 12)
- ❑ (13, 12)
- ❑ (13, 14)
- ❑ (12, 14)
- ❑ (12, 13)
- ❑ (11, 13)
- ❑ (11, 17)

Line 5
- ❑ (18, 14)
- ❑ (16, 14)
- ❑ (18, 15)
- ❑ (18, 13)
- ❑ (20, 10)
- ❑ (16, 10)
- ❑ (18, 13)

Line 6
- ❑ (8, 1)
- ❑ (8, 3)
- ❑ (9, 4)
- ❑ (12, 4)
- ❑ (13, 3)
- ❑ (13, 1)

Line 7
- ❑ (17, 10)
- ❑ (17, 6)
- ❑ (16, 6)
- ❑ (16, 7)
- ❑ (15, 7)
- ❑ (15, 15)
- ❑ (13, 15)
- ❑ (13, 16)
- ❑ (15, 16

Line 8
- ❑ (11, 14)
- ❑ (10, 14)
- ❑ (10, 13)
- ❑ (9, 13)
- ❑ (9, 14)
- ❑ (8, 14)

Line 9
- ❑ (11, 9)
- ❑ (10, 9)
- ❑ (10, 11)
- ❑ (11, 11))
- ❑ (11, 9)

Line 10
- ❑ (15, 15)
- ❑ (15, 17)
- ❑ (11, 17)
- ❑ (13, 20)
- ❑ (15, 17

Line 11
- ❑ (19, 10)
- ❑ (19, 8)
- ❑ (18, 8)
- ❑ (18, 9)
- ❑ (19,9)
- ❑ (19, 1)
- ❑ (18, 0)
- ❑ (17, 0)
- ❑ (16, 1)
- ❑ (5, 1)
- ❑ (4, 0)
- ❑ (3, 0)
- ❑ (2, 1)
- ❑ (2, 9)

Line 12
- ❑ (7, 7)
- ❑ (7, 6)
- ❑ (8, 6)
- ❑ (8, 7)
- ❑ (10, 7)
- ❑ (10, 6)
- ❑ (11, 6)
- ❑ (11, 7)
- ❑ (12, 7)

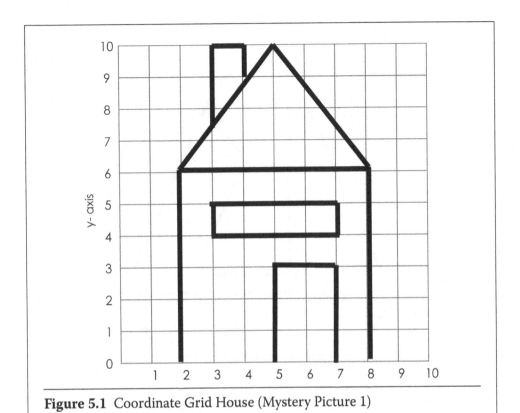

Figure 5.1 Coordinate Grid House (Mystery Picture 1)

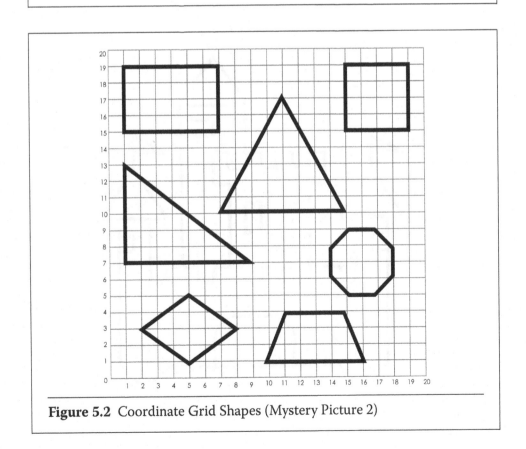

Figure 5.2 Coordinate Grid Shapes (Mystery Picture 2)

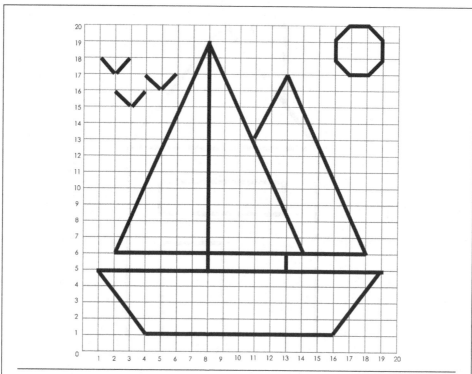

Figure 5.3 Coordinate Grid Sailboat (Mystery Picture 3)

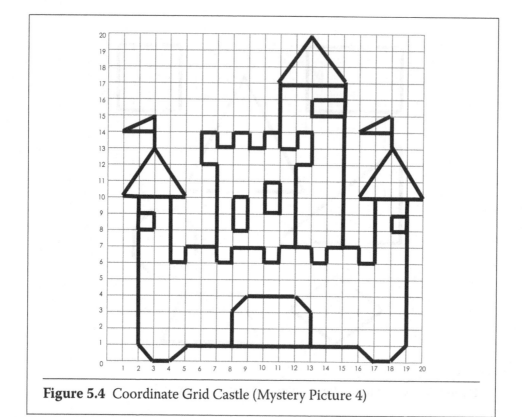

Figure 5.4 Coordinate Grid Castle (Mystery Picture 4)

the coordinate pairs. This picture will be created by locating the first coordinate and then connecting it with straight lines to the rest of the coordinates for the section.

❏ Model labeling the first and second points and using a ruler to connect the dots. Model crossing off the coordinate pairs as you go. This will help keep the students on track.

❏ If students understand the concept, they may complete the rest of the picture on their own. However, you may need to continue modeling and checking student work for this first mystery picture.

❏ There are three more coordinate mystery pictures which increase in difficulty. You may wish to assign these according to student readiness, or you may let them choose. To avoid frustration, we recommend only allowing students to choose the fourth mystery picture after they have successfully completed at least two of the easier ones.

Seeking Structure Lesson 2: The Four-Color Theorem

Objective: Explore how maps organize visual information by proving the Four-Color Theorem.

Materials

❏ *There's a Map on My Lap* by Tish Rabe (teacher's copy)
❏ Handout 5.5: Read Aloud Reflection (one per student)
❏ Handout 5.6: Seeking Structure Mini-Booklet (four pages) (one per student)
❏ Handout 5.7: US Map (one per student)

Whole Group Introduction

❏ Remind students that our brains look for structure in patterns.
❏ Display the bottom half of Handout 5.5. Explain that in this lesson, "maps" will be geometrical shapes and regions to color.
❏ Tell students, "Let's suppose you started working for a map-making company and your job is to color in the blank maps. Your task is to color the countries so that no two adjacent countries share the same color and to use the least number of colors possible."
❏ Ask students to brainstorm strategies and theories on how to accomplish this task.

Read Aloud Activity

❏ Tell students they are going to read a book about maps. Read aloud the book *There's a Map on My Lap* by Tish Rabe. This book introduces different types of maps, their formats, and the tools we use to read maps.

❏ Distribute the Read Aloud Reflection page (Handout 5.5). Direct students to carefully consider and answer the questions on the top half. Allow students to talk in pairs or small groups. When students have finished, discuss responses as a whole group.

❏ Direct students to the bottom half of the page, and tell them to determine the fewest colors they will need to color this map. Tell students to color a small dot in each section to determine placement. Then, once they have determined their answer, they may color the section in completely.

Box 5.2: *There's a Map on My Lap* Key Understandings

❏ *There's a Map on My Lap* teaches all about cartography and the uses of various maps.

❏ The various maps all have structures. For example, there are latitude and longitude lines to help with coordinates. There is a scale to determine actual distance. Topical maps use colors to show the heights of the region.

Skill Development Activity

Teacher's note: Prepare the Seeking Structure Mini-Booklet (Handout 5.6) for each student.

❏ Fold the front/back cover in half. The crease should be on the left side of the front cover.

❏ Fold each of the inner pages in half with the text facing outward. The crease should be on the right side of the even-numbered pages.

❏ Stack folded book pages so that even page numbers are stacked sequentially facing the top, starting with page 2.

Handout 5.5: Read Aloud Reflection

There's a Map on My Lap by Tish Rabe

Name: _____

Summarize the main idea of the story.	How did the book show structure?

Follow the rules of "map" coloring to fill in this map with the fewest colors.

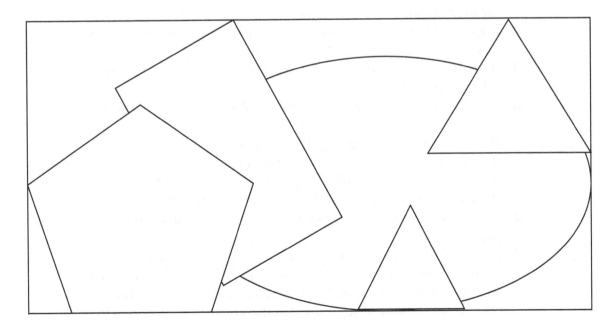

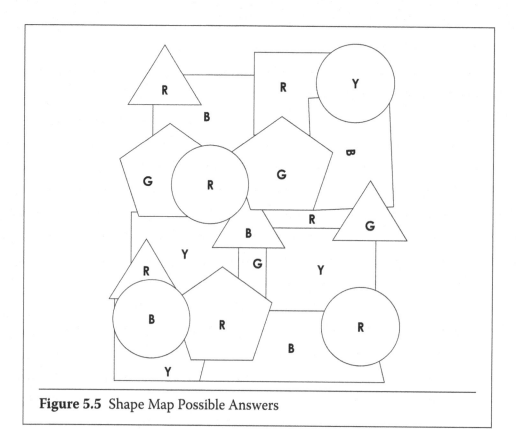

Figure 5.5 Shape Map Possible Answers

❏ Place the stack of folded interior pages inside of the folded cover page. Loose edges should be against the cover's fold, with the creased edge of the internal pages facing outward.
❏ Staple along the left-hand side, using the provided staple lines as a guide.
❏ If desired, place a strip of tape along the left-hand side to cover the staples, trimming any excess.
❏ Distribute the Seeking Structure Mini-Booklets. Explain the directions for map coloring.
  ■ Each region should get exactly one color.
  ■ Use the fewest number of colors possible.
  ■ When two regions touch along a side, they must be different colors.
  ■ The corners of each region may touch the same color.
❏ Read the booklet together as you model how to color in the regions on page 2.
❏ Next, explain to students that mathematicians have long debated the theory that no more than four colors are required to color the regions on a map so that no two regions sharing a boundary will have the same color. However, some mathematicians don't believe this theorem to be

Patterns and
Repetitions
which don't
break become
RULES!

SEEKING STRUCTURE

LOOKING FOR REPETITION
AND PATTERNS

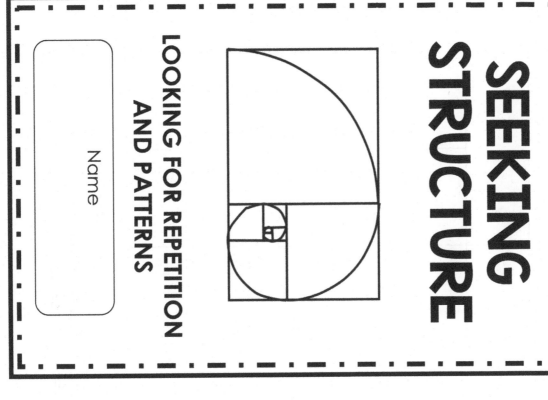

Name

Directions for Map Coloring

- Each region should get exactly one color.

- Use the fewest number of colors possible.

- When two regions touch along a side, they must be different colors.

- The corners of each region may touch the same color.

What is the least number of colors you can use to color each region so that no two regions which share a side touch?

1

2

What do you notice about these maps?

What is the least number of colors you can use to color each region so that no two regions which share a side touch?

The Four-Color Theorem

states that **only four colors** are required to **color ANY map** such that no 2 adjacent regions. However, some mathematicians don't believe this theorem to be true, as it is only proven through exhaustion, not an actual algorithm. Meaning, this theory has not been disproven, therefore it is believed to be true.

What do you think? Can you prove or disprove the theorem?

Prove the Four-Color Theorem
Shape Map

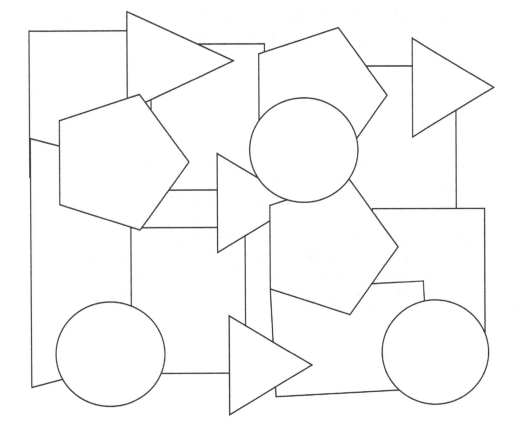

What structures do you notice when proving this theorem?

true, as it is only proven through exhaustion, not an actual algorithm—meaning that this theory has not been disproven, and therefore it is believed to be true.

❏ Direct students to look at page 3. Ask students, "What strategies can you think of to color this Shape Map?"

❏ Model planning out the colors by putting a small colored dot in the corner of each shape.

❏ At this time, you may introduce the Greedy Algorithm, which is a technique where you color as much as you can with one color before switching to the next color.

❏ Allow students to complete the rest of the booklet.

❏ Optional Extension: Show students the US map page from the book *There's a Map on My Lap* by Tish Rabe. Ask students how many colors were used to color in this map. Ask students if they think that it's necessary to use five colors.

❏ Give each student or pair of students a copy of the blackline US map (Handout 5.7). Tell students they are to prove or disprove the Four-Color Theorem: Every map can be colored using just four colors such that no two areas may touch another area with the same color.

Seeking Structure Authentic Application Activity: Euler's Circuits

Objective: Apply structure to create rules.

Materials

❏ Handout 5.8: Read Aloud Reflection (one per student)
❏ Konigsberg Bridge Problem Video
  ▪ https://ed.ted.com/lessons/how-the-konigsberg-bridge-problem -changed-mathematics-dan-van-der-vieren
❏ Handout 5.9: The Bridge to Graph Theory (one per student)
❏ Handout 5.10: Graph Theory Anchor Chart (one enlarged for the class)
❏ Handout 5.11: Euler Paths Discovery (one per student)
❏ Handout 5.12: Creating Eulerian Paths (one per student)

Handout 5.7: Three Color Shading

Name: _____

Read Aloud Activity

❏ Remind students that seeking structure means looking for patterns and repetitions. Explain that when a pattern doesn't break, that becomes a rule. For example, the months of the year always occur in the same pattern, which makes their order a rule.

❏ Tell students that throughout the next lessons, they will discover mathematical rules that were discovered by analyzing the structure of patterns.

❏ Tell students that this book will use many of the terms they have learned throughout this unit. Remind students to pay close attention to the patterns and structures in this text.

❏ Read aloud *Sir Cumference and the Sword in the Cone* by Cindy Neuschwander. In this book, students will try to solve the king's riddle using mathematical structures.

❏ Hand out the Read Aloud Reflection (Handout 5.8).

❏ Walk students through the questions. Encourage students to put into words the patterns, repetitions, and structures of the book, e.g., Euler's law is a structure because the equation of Faces + Vertices – Straight Edges always equals 2.

❏ Bring out the 3D shapes created in the Exploring Dimension section earlier in the unit. Walk students through completing Table 5.2.

Box 5.3: *Sir Cumference and the Sword in the Cone* Key Understandings

This book shows geometrical structures throughout. First, they introduce the concept of nets—flattened-out 3D figures. Next, they fold the nets into 3D figures. They discuss the numbers of faces, points, and edges on each figure. Using all this knowledge, the men uncover Euler's Law (when the number of faces of a geometric solid is added to the number of its vertices, and then the number of its edges is subtracted, the answer will always be 2).

Skill Development: Authentic Application

❏ Tell students that mathematician Leonhard Euler also made other mathematical discoveries. Through this next section they will learn about Graph Theory.

Handout 5.8: Read Aloud Reflection

Sir Cumference and the Sword in the Cone by Cindy Neuschwander

Name: _____

| How did the story use the **structures** of geometry? | Explain Euler's Law. |

Complete the chart below to discover if Euler's law always is true.

SHAPE	FLAT FACES	VERTICES	FACES + VERTICES	STRAIGHT EDGES	F + P − E =
pentagonal prism					
pentagonal pyramid					
hexagonal prism					
hexagonal pyramid					
octahedron					
dodecahedron					

TABLE 5.2

Euler's Law (Handout 7.8) Answer Key

Shape	Flat Faces	Vertices	Faces + Vertices	Straight Edges	F + P – E =
pentagonal prism	7	10	17	15	2
pentagonal pyramid	6	6	12	10	2
hexagonal prism	8	12	20	18	2
hexagonal pyramid	7	7	14	12	2
octahedron	8	6	14	12	2
dodecahedron	12	20	32	30	2

❏ Distribute The Bridge to Graph Theory (Handout 5.9). Direct students to the top three maps. Tell students that they are to imagine that each circle is a city and that each dotted line is a road. The goal is to trace a path to cross each road only one time. They may start at any dot. Allow students time to work and then ask for volunteers to model their paths. Encourage students to share their observations, paths, and strategies.

❏ Next, read the information on the Konigsberg Bridge. Encourage students to try and trace the path through the town of Konigsberg, visiting each part of the town and crossing each road only once. After students have tried various paths (about 5 minutes), explain that mathematician Leonhard Euler proved there is no solution to the problem.

❏ Show students the Graph Theory Anchor Chart (Handout 5.10). Explain that in Graph Theory, the circles are called *vertices* (or points) and the dotted lines are called *edges* (lines). The *degree of edges* is the number of edges "lines" touching each vertex.

 ■ *Euler paths* must travel through every edge once and only once and the starting point and ending point are different vertices.

 ■ An *Euler circuit* is an Euler path that begins and ends at the same vertex.

❏ Distribute Euler Path Discovery (Handout 5.11). Model completing the first path and completing the chart accordingly. Next, allow students to

Handout 5.9: The Bridge to Graph Theory

Name: _____

Look at the "maps" of dots and dotted lines. Imagine each dot is a city and each dotted line is a road. Trace a way to cross each road only one time. You may start at any dot.

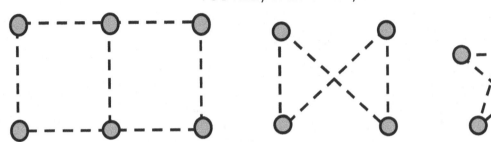

What do you notice about these "maps"?

The Konigsberg Bridge

In the 1700's the people from Konigsberg, Germany challenged one another to travel through the town visiting each labeled point by crossing each bridge just once.

Use the modified map below. Can you trace a path through the town, visiting each part of the town and only traveling down each road only once?

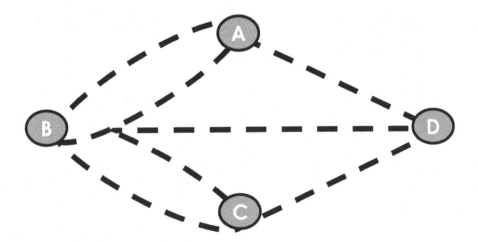

Did you find a path?

Don't worry, if you couldn't find a path. There isn't one! Leonhard Euler proved this to be true in 1736 and in doing so created Graph Theory. The study of how things are connected.

GRAPH THEORY
the study of how things are connected

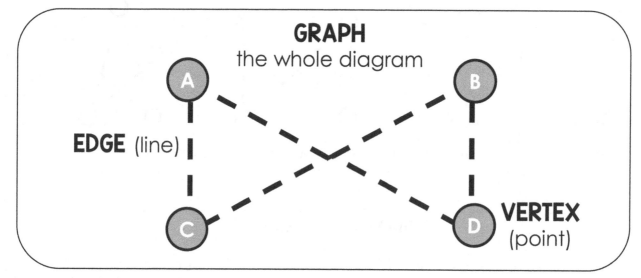

GRAPH
the whole diagram

EDGE (line)

VERTEX (point)

DEGREE (number of edges that lead to a vertex)
Vertex A, B, C, and D all have 2 degrees.

EULER PATH

Must travel through every edge once and only once and starts and ends at a different vertices.

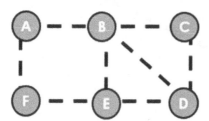

EULER CIRCUIT

A Euler path that starts and ends at the same vertex.

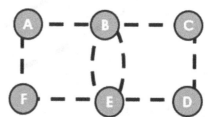

Handout 5.11: Euler Paths Discovery

Complete the chart on the shapes below to see if you can uncover the theory of Euler's Paths?

1

2

3

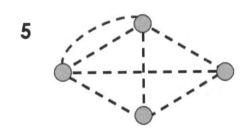

4

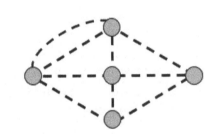

5

6

Shape	Euler Path?	Dots (Vertices)	How many with even degrees?	How many with odd degrees?
1				
2				
3				
4				
5				
6				

What patterns do you notice?

work individually, in pairs, or in a small group. Tell students they must complete the chart for each graph.

❏ After students have completed the chart, encourage them to find patterns in their charts. Guide students to discover that to make an Euler path, the number of odd vertices must be two or zero.

Shape	Euler path?	Dots (vertices)	How many with even degrees?	How many with odd degrees?
1	yes	4	4	0
2	yes	4	2	2
3	no	5	1	4
4	no	4	0	4
5	yes	4	2	2
6	yes	5	3	2

❏ Play the Ted Talk: *How the Königsberg Bridge Problem Changed Mathematics.* This short video explains the entire process of determining Eulerian paths.

❏ Finally, distribute Create your own Eulerian paths (Handout 5.12). Encourage students to challenged themselves to create graphs with many degrees.

Seeking Structure Concluding Activities

❏ Distribute the Seeking Structure Exit Ticket (Appendix A). Ask students to reflect on their learning about the skill of looking for repetitions and patterns. Allow time for students to complete the exit ticket. Use this as a formative assessment to gain a better understanding of your students' readiness to effectively practice the skills of seeking structure.

❏ If desired, complete the Group Seeking Structure Rubric (Appendix A) to track students' progress with the skill.

❏ If desired, use the Visual-Spatial Thinking Student Observation Rubric (Appendix A) to assess and quantify individual students' mastery.

❏ Ask students to retrieve their Visual-Spatial Thinking Avatar (Handout I.3). In the Seeking Structure box, they should either write the main ideas of this section or illustrate their avatar using the skills of looking for repetitions and patterns.

Handout 5.12: Creating Eulerian Paths

Without tracing, determine if the following graphs have a Euler's path?

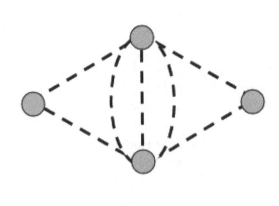 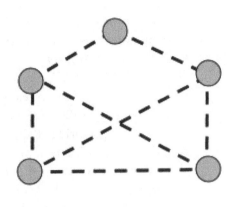

_____   _____

Your turn: Create four Euler Paths of your own. Try to create one with 7 roads.

Bibliography

5.6 *Euler Paths and Cycles-Penn Math* (March 16, 2016). https://www2.math .upenn.edu/~mlazar/math170/notes05-6.pdf.

Glass, J. (1998). *A fly on the ceiling.* New York. Scholastic.

Levin, O. (2013–2017). Graph theory. In *Discrete mathematics: An open introduction.* http://discrete.openmathbooks.org/dmoi2/ch_graphtheory.html

Neuschwande, D. (2003). *Sir Cumference and the sword in the cone.* Watertown, MA: Charlesbridge Publishing.

Rabe, T. (2002). *There's a map on my lap!* New York: Random House.

Van der Vieren, D. (n.d.). *How the Königsberg bridge problem changed Mathematics* [video]. *TEDEd.* https://ed.ted.com/lessons/how-the-konigsberg-bridge-problem-changed-mathematics-dan-van-der-vieren.

Appendix A

Assessments

Several assessment options are provided in this unit. It is not necessary to use all the options provided; rather, you should choose the options that work best for your own classroom needs.

One aspect to pay close attention to is the indicators associated with each thinking skill. These indicators provide an outline of expected behavioral outcomes for students. As you work through the lessons, keep an eye out for students who are able to achieve the indicators efficiently and effectively, as well as those who may need more support. The intent of this unit is to foster a mastery mindset; make note of student growth and skill development as you progress, rather than focusing on summative outcomes against specific benchmarks.

1. **Exit Tickets:** Exit tickets are provided to correspond with each sub-skill. These are intended to be formative, giving you a sense of students' mastery and self-efficacy with each skill. These tickets will also give you great insight into areas where a re-visit is warranted. If a student would benefit from additional instruction in a sub-skill area, consider using one or more of the extension options listed in Appendix B.
2. **Individual Student Observations:** This form is intended for use for each student individually. All five thinking skills are outlined on the page, and you can track individual student progress toward indicator

goals easily. Use this form to gather data, report data to stakeholders, or simply help students see their own progress.

3. **Visual-Spatial Thinking Sub-Skill Group Observation Checklists:** This checklist is provided for each thinking skill. This is a great running measure of students' mastery of the indicators associated with each thinking skill. Each skill has three indicators for mastery, and you can track student progress toward these goals as a group using this form.

4. **Symmetry Quilt Rubric for Assessment:** Provided here is a rubric for assessment after completion of symmetry quilt project in Sub-Skill 1.